Nation Makers
the Art of Self-Government

Let every soul be subject to the governing authorities. For there is no authority except from God, and the authorities that exist are appointed by God. Therefore whoever resists the authority resists the ordinance of God, and those who resist will bring judgment on themselves.

Romans 13:1–2
[New King James Version]

God grant that in America true religion and civil liberty may be inseparable, and that the unjust attempts to destroy the one may in the issue tend to the support and establishment of both.

Rev. John Witherspoon
[signer of the Declaration of Independence, Fast Day Sermon of May 17, 1776, called for by Congress.]

Where the Spirit of the Lord is, there is liberty.
II Corinthians 3:17

The Foundation for American Christian Education
Chesapeake, Virginia

Nation Makers
the Art of Self-Government

by Rosalie J. Slater and Verna M. Hall

Originally *Rudiments of America's Christian History and Government*
First Edition, Copyright June 1, 1968

Second revised edition, copyright July 20, 1994
Second Printing 2008
Edited by Carole G. Adams

Third Revised Edition, Copyright May 8, 2017
by The Foundation for American Christian Education
Edited by Carole G. Adams

ISBN 978-1-935851-24-0
Cover painting
Nation Makers by Howard Pyle

Published by

The Foundation for American Christian Education
P.O. Box 9588, Chesapeake, Virginia 23321-9588
800-352-3223 • FACE.net

Introduction

by the Authors, Rosalie J. Slater and Verna M. Hall 1968

Verna M. Hall researched and published the ideas that directed our Founding Fathers in their quest for self-government. Ms. Hall documented her findings from original historic sources that identify the root of American liberty. She was joined by Rosalie J. Slater who identified the historic method of education that formed American minds and hearts in the first 200 years of her history. The following is the original introduction to the course.

The knowledge of our American history is so important to Americans that without it we act like a nation that has lost its memory. Knowledge of America's Christian History both restores our national memory and provides us with the purpose for which America was established.

Historians who wrote close to the period of our founding were convinced that God reserved this continent and held it in readiness for that time when mankind was ready to accept to the fullest the opportunity and the responsibility for extending Christian liberty to every sphere of life. No other nation in the Christian era has had such a unique establishment as America. No other nation has consciously and purposely based its institutions upon Christian Biblical principles. There would be no America if there were no Christianity.

Few Christians in America really know America's Christian History. Yet no one has destroyed the record. Rather it has been forgotten and neglected by the very people who should love this tremendous testimony of Christ His Story in America. Now, after more than 100 years of gradually turning away from our original Christian purpose and founding, once again Americans can read for themselves the documentation in the "original" sources of our history. The journals of the Continental Congress, the journals of the individual colonial legislatures, governmental proclamations, diplomatic correspondence, letters, speeches, sermons, and newspapers of the times, all reveal the Christian History of our nation.

If you are one of those young American Christians still in school who has not yet learned what America is all about, this course will help you. It is designed to show that the history of Christianity and the history of America cannot be separated. It restores to our nation the purpose for which God brought her into being—tracing the Chain of Christianity® moving westward.

Historians of today look at America's early history through the lenses of contemporary philosophies of government and they fail to understand the reasoning of her Founders. A major purpose for this course is to restore the Christian writing and Biblical reasoning of those individuals who were closer to that period when America was identifying herself as a separate nation. If we are to appreciate the sacred trust of Christian government, we must understand it in the context of a Bible-loving and a Bible-living people.

Our first selection for this course in the "rudiments" of Christian self-government is from Noah Webster's *Letters to a Young Gentleman Commencing His Education*. In order that you might better appreciate who is writing these letters, we have prepared a short biography of Mr. Webster—one of the most important of the Founding Fathers for you to know. He built the foundation for American Christian education upon the cornerstone of Jesus Christ. "For other foundation can no man lay than that is laid, which is Jesus Christ." [1 Corinthians 3:11]

Acknowledgments

As a Christian high school teacher, I was invited to tour the "F.A.C.E. Demonstration School" in Hanford, California where I had the privilege of observing the teachers, among them Mr. James Rose and Ms. Kathy Dang. The "Rudiments of America's Christian History and Government" class taught by Ms. Beth Ballenger is still vivid in memory. In the classroom, I witnessed seventh graders discussing self-government and Christian character as essential to liberty, using such language as "self aggrandizement" as they searched the Bible and the original Webster *American Dictionary of the English Language.*

The method of education that forged the character of liberty in early America thrived in that classroom. The discussion could have occurred in a colonial classroom at Harvard College, or at a town hall meeting in Boston, or in the House of Burgesses in Williamsburg. Certainly the same discussion should be occurring routinely today if we are to stand fast in liberty and "not submit again to a yoke of bondage."

Rosalie Slater and Verna Hall, mentors at large to many, captured, documented, and proved the "idea of America" to be a Christian idea. Christians owe much to their prescient work. In Ms. Hall's last years, she labored over the Biblical Foundations of the Constitution planning to make it "CHOC III"; though never edited for publishing, the complete manuscript is archived in the Hall-Slater Library in Chesapeake. In it we find the influence of the theologian of the American Republic, William Ames. In *Nation Makers*, we include Peter Ramus and William Ames whose influence in the founding of the American Republic has been too long abandoned, and whose work provides us building tools for restoring the Christian "idea of America" in fulfillment of Ms. Hall's vision.

The truths proffered by the original Rudiments course belong in the hearts and minds of all young Americans. With that conviction, we offer a revision of the original course enhanced for the student and teacher. Along with the original text published in 1968, the revision named *Nation Makers: the Art of Self-Government* includes the required excerpts of the "red books" to ensure the convenient flow of the topics. It also includes charts, narrative, and study helps for the support of instruction.

We at F.A.C.E. follow in the steps of the many teachers and parents who taught the Rudiments course. We extend gratitude also to our teacher, Mr. Ben Gilmore, whose "Principles of American Government" course has been invaluable to us, and who contributed to this book. We are grateful for the research and writing Rebecca H. Beach, our lead scholar and teacher of Ramus and Ames. The Rudiments course endured and impacted the nation for fifty years. It is our prayer that the revision will take the course into many future generations. The text of the original *Rudiments* book is enlarged by narrative written by the editor, and by Carey Adams-Dudkovsky and Ben Gilmore, inserted to enhance understanding of the original concepts.

Carole Adams, May 8, 2017

NATION MAKERS: THE ART OF SELF-GOVERNMENT

Table of Contents

Introduction...3
Acknowledgments..4
Table of Contents 5
Purpose and Goal of the Course...7
    Objectives for Teachers and Students 8
    Preview of Nation Makers 9

The Necessity of Christian Character.......................................11
    EDUCATION FORMS CHARACTER 13
        The Founding Father of American Scholarship and Education..........13
        A Word about Primary Sources 18
    CHARACTER FORMS A FREE OR A FETTERED LIFE 19
        The Individual Character and How Men Are Governed 19
            Individual Responsibilities....................................20
            Individual Duties..21
        Living by Standards 24
            The Commandments Chart and Part I Essay.......................32
            American Education Models 33
        Part I Essay...37

The Blessing of Self-Government 39
    GOD'S PRINCIPLE OF INDIVIDUALITY 41
    PROVIDENTIAL HISTORY 45
        Understanding God's Hand in Human History 48
        Nation Making Methods and Results.................................50
        A Model of Providential History: Creation.........................52
        Individual Links on the Chain of Christianity®....................55
        Part II Essay: "The Hand of God in Human History".................58

The Nature of Law...59
    NATURAL LAW AND REVEALED LAW 60
        Laws of Nature and of Nature's God................................61
    MORAL LAW AND THE PREPARATION FOR CHRIST 64

CIVIL LAW AND NATION MAKING 72
   Pagan Elements in History 72
   Nation Making by Slavery: Greek Democracy 77
   Centralization through Law: Roman Republic. 79
   Representation in America 82
   Two Systems of Law: Roman and Common 84
   Part III Essay: "The Role of Representation in the 'Idea of America'" 85

The Impact of Christ on Religion, Education and Government 87
REFORM OF RELIGION 89
   John Wycliffe 89
   Martin Luther 92
   John Calvin 95
   The Story of the Bible in English. 97
   The Martyrdom of William Tyndale 98
REFORM OF EDUCATION. 102
REFORM OF LAW & GOVERNMENT 104
   English Constitutional Law: Liberty under Law. 104
      Magna Charta – 1215 105
      Petition of Right – 1628. 106
      Rights and Liberties. 109
CHRISTIAN PHILOSOPHERS AND CONSTITUTIONAL GOVERNMENT 115
   John Locke 115
   Charles de Montesquieu. 117
   William Blackstone. 119
   Part IV Essay: "Natural Law and Revealed Law: How the Reform of Religion, Education, Law, and Government Affected the Founding of America" 122

America—The Fullest Expression of a Christian Nation 123
THE PARENT COLONIES. 125
   Virginia. 126
   New England 130
THE THEOLOGY OF THE AMERICAN REPUBLIC. 133
   The Pastor, the Pulpit, and American Liberty. 134
   Restoring the "Idea of America:" the Pulpit 138
RESTORING CHRISTIAN CHARACTER AND SELF-GOVERNMENT 139
   An American Christian Education. 139
   Words Have Consequences 140
   Final Essay: "Education and the American Republic". 141

Howard Pyle 142
Bibliography 143
Index of Images 144

Purpose and Goal of "Nation Makers" Course

Nation Makers: the Art of Self-Government teaches the "idea of America:" the vision and principles that formed the first self-governing nation in the history of the world.

The idea of a self-governing nation emerged from man's quest for liberty. The idea of a self-governing nation drove the Pilgrims to pass "a sea of troubles...to...a desolate wilderness, full of wild beasts and wild men." The idea of a self-governing nation drove the patriots of the thirteen colonies to study government and its source in the Scriptures; it drove the pastors of the Colonial pulpits to teach their parishioners the theology of liberty; and it drove the farmers and shopkeepers illustrated on our cover to war against the most powerful army in the world. The idea of a self-governing nation drove the abolitionists, the Confederates of the 1860's, the soldiers on the beaches of Normandy, and those who immigrated to these shores from places of tyranny and oppression.

The "idea of America" is obscured today by the forgetfulness of Americans. How does one forget an idea that is so ardently pursued and hard-won? History is driven by ideas, but history is forgotten when it is not taught. When parents and teachers neglect the duty of teaching children the mighty acts of God, that void of ignorance is readily filled with a false view of history which in turn leaves no place for the knowledge of God's glory.

Why does the "idea of America" have power to call forth the sacrifice of so many so consistently over so many years? Is it because of one sentence that captures the "idea?"

> We hold these truths to be self-evident, that all men are created equal,
> that they are endowed by their Creator with certain unalienable Rights that
> among these are Life, Liberty, and the Pursuit of Happiness.

This remarkable sentence, written over 240 years ago, has power in every generation because it says a nation should be founded upon Truth – self-evident Truth that was true, is true, and will remain true for all people at all times in all places. It is a Truth that cannot be disproved and that existed from Creation.

What is the source of this Truth? What evidence can we see? How did this Truth come to us? What are we to do with it?

The purpose and goal of the *Nation Makers: the Art of Self-Government* is inculcating the "idea of America" in the hearts and minds of young Americans today by addressing those questions thoughtfully, and lingering reflectively in them to form a full understanding of the wisdom needed by each generation to sustain the American Republic.

The content of the course is dependent upon these texts:

- The Bible, usually the ESV, often the New King James Version
- *American Dictionary of the English Language*, 1828, Noah Webster
- *Teaching and Learning America's Christian History: the Principle Approach*, R. J. Slater
- *The Christian History of the Constitution of the United States of America: Christian Self-Government*, V. M. Hall
- "The Education of John Quincy Adams: the Character for a Christian Republic," Slater in *The Christian History of the American Revolution: Consider and Ponder*, V.M. Hall

Nation Makers:
the Art of Self-Government

OBJECTIVES FOR TEACHERS AND STUDENTS

Governing Purpose—Mastering the "idea of America", and internalizing the principles of living well and living free in the Christian Constitutional Republic, by understanding fully and articulating clearly the following major points and their supporting concepts:

- How America is unique among nations
- Two basic outcomes of studying *Nation Makers*

I. The Necessity of Christian Character to the Republic
    a. The nature of authentic American education
    b. The contribution of Founding Father Noah Webster to the Republic
    c. The essentials of education for forming the character of self-government
    d. The nature of Christian character as the foundation of living well and free
    e. How the quality of character forms the individual life
    f. What constitutes individual responsibility and duty
    g. The nature of natural law and revealed law: the Commandments
    h. Living out the revealed law by practicing its standards in real life
    i. How the various forms of American education today answer the three questions posed by Noah Webster: Who made me? Why was I made? What is my duty?

II. The Blessing of Self-Government
    a. The big picture: providence and principles
    b. The design of creation and how it serves God's purposes: the theater of history
    c. The Hand of God in human history
    d. Types of nation making in history
    e. The connection between Christianity and America

III. Natural Law and Revealed Law
    a. The nature and use of law
    b. Moral law and its fulfillment
    c. The history of civil law
    d. Two systems of law

IV. The Impact of Christ on History, Education and Government
    a. The reform of religion
    b. The reform of education
    c. The reform of government
    d. Governing documents reflect the progress of liberty with law

V. America—The Fullest Expression of a Christian Nation
    a. The legacy of the parent colonies
    b. The theology of the parent colonies
    c. The role of the church and clergy in the formation of the "idea of America"
    d. Restoring the American Republic today

Preview of Nation Makers

Nation Makers: the Art of Self-Government tells the story of the men and women who brought about the "idea of America" as their love of God enlightened their understanding of his law, the Gospel of Christ, and God's government of His universe.

Most nations that ever existed were formed on the basis of racial or ethnic affinities. China is a nation of Chinese with a common gene pool and cultural bonds. But America is the only nation that was birthed not by racial or ethnic necessities, not by aristocracy or oligarchy, but solely by the power of the idea of "living to God" by subjecting civil and religious liberty to His revealed law. It has been said that God chose Israel, but America chose God.

The heroic story of America began in ancient times in the mind of God who placed man at liberty in the Garden of Eden. Recorded history beginning with the Bible shows man's resistance to God and its enslaving consequences, man's redemption through the Gospel, and man's struggle to regain freedom. Throughout history various tyrants–kings, caesars, princes, pharaohs, masters, despots, overlords, emperors, shahs, moguls, dukes, doges, sultans, czars, lords, sheiks, dictators – governed and subjected their people, often malevolently.

After many millennia when slavery was commonly practiced worldwide with its ensuing miseries, God used the Gospel of Christ not only to free man from sin, but to make man wise in governing himself without oppression. The providential view of history culminates in the U.S. Constitution affording Americans the greatest freedom and prosperity ever experienced by any group of people in the world.

Our story is the story of people and events but ultimately the story of an idea—the capacity of mankind to govern himself, without a king or a ruler, with liberty of conscience and with the right to life and property. Those soldiers depicted on the cover of this book, who bled and died for the "idea of America," teach us again several generations later, to cherish that Christian idea.

The topics and major principles of the "idea of America" in the diagram below are to be fixed in memory to frame your study.

Topics to be Mastered	Corresponding Principles
Nation Makers: the Art of Self-Government → The necessity of Christian character / The blessing of self-government	Christianity produces liberty → Liberty is first internal / Self-government limits external control

Record the governing purpose, the two diagrams of the topics, and corresponding principles in your notebook.

Icon Key

Chat Write

Essay Definition

Nation Makers is presented in five sections that each represent the thinking contained in the "idea of America." You will learn each of the five concepts and the arguments that support them. Memorize the titles of the five sections.

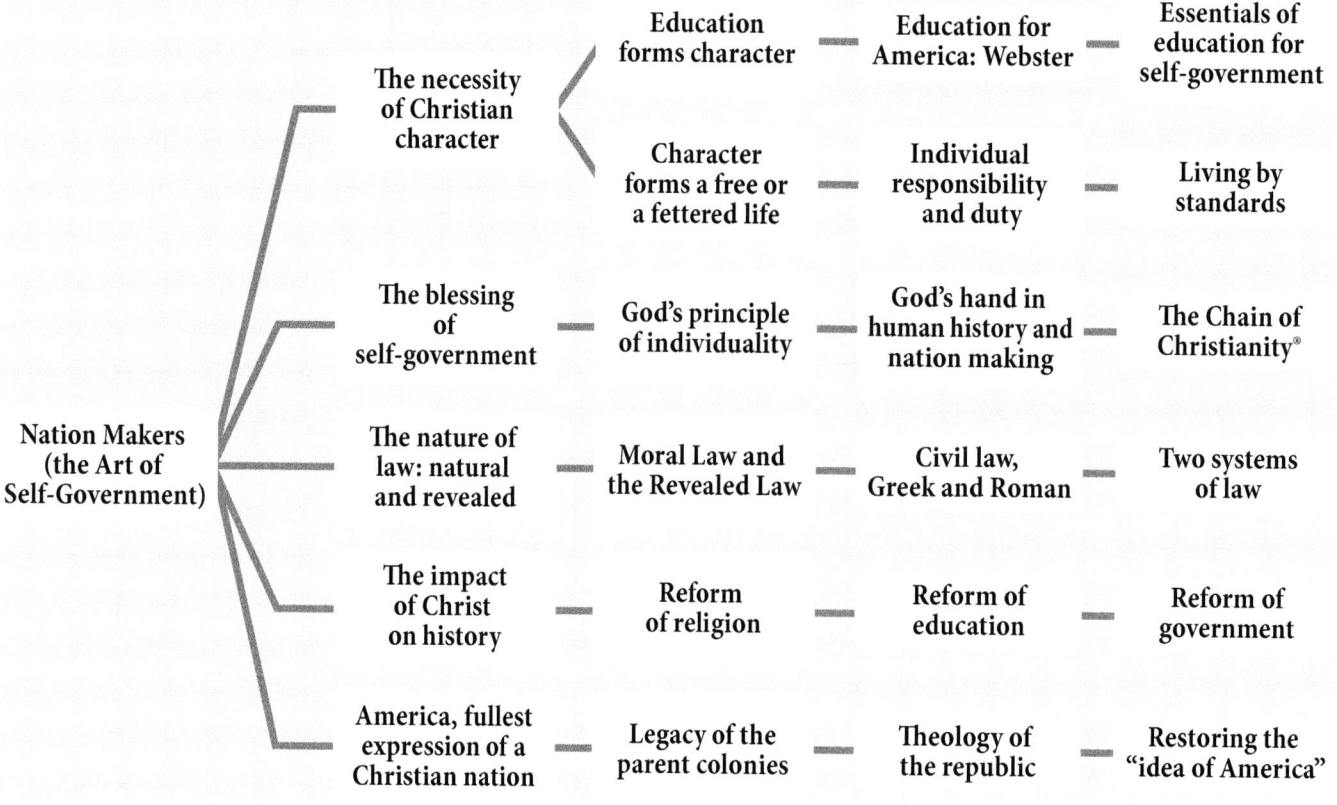

What do you think? By examining the chart you can see:

- The themes and topics of the "idea of America."
- Upon what the necessity of Christian character is dependent.
- Why Christian character is a necessity for self-government.
- What is the impact of Christ on history.
- What is the key to restoring the Republic.

Nation Makers
Part I:
The Necessity of Christian Character

| Education forms character | Education for America | Essentials of education for self-government |

The Necessity of Christian Character

By knowing history one gains wisdom. By understanding government, both internal and external, one prepares to enjoy a happy, fulfilling life. For the student, the study of Nation Makers imparts wisdom in two beneficial ways:

- **Preparing you to live a life of personal liberty**
- **Preparing you to lead your generation in sustaining the "idea of America"**

How do you approach the study of an idea? The study of ideas calls for careful thinking and debate. The process of understanding an idea begins with testing the idea to be convinced of its value and application. History demonstrates and celebrates the consequence of the "idea of America" over the last 250 years. History also shows us how the "idea of America" developed into a Republic that not only affords liberty to the individual but also became a beacon of liberty and hope to a world ravaged by a range of tyrannies.

The history of America shows how an idea residing internally in the hearts of many became an external expression that would be used of God to bless the world and people everywhere. It is the story of Christian self-government and its manifestation in the American Republic. It begins in Part I with the internal aspect: Christian character. In Parts II–V of the study we will see the impact the "idea of America" made externally upon history.

Two principles form the necessity of Christian character to the Republic:

(1) Education forms character; (2) Christianity produces liberty.

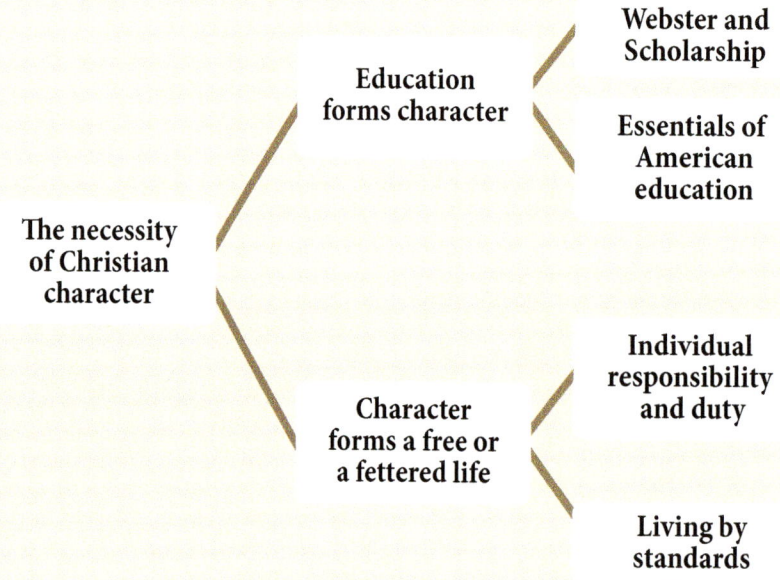

 *What is the internal aspect of the "idea of America?"*

Record the Memory Tree of "The Necessity of Christian Character" above in your notebook.

Education Forms Character

The Founding Father of American Scholarship and Education

Who was Noah Webster? Or, rather, who is Noah Webster in relation to American Christian education? Most of us associate the name of Webster with the Dictionary. Noah Webster was the first American to produce *An American Dictionary of the English Language*. But the Webster dictionary was only one part of a larger plan of American Christian education that Noah Webster worked at for more than sixty years.

No single American has contributed so much to American education as has Noah Webster. Yet today few students in American schools are aware of their heritage of American Christian education through the contributions—and the life and testimony—of Noah Webster. Before an inheritance can bless its beneficiaries it must be claimed. And, by the same token, we have to be able to identify our inheritance, to recognize it, before we can claim it for our own.

All the definitions you will ponder in this course are from Noah Webster's first edition of An American Dictionary of the English Language, published as facsimile of the 1828 original by the Foundation for American Christian Education.

> HER′ITAGE, n. [Fr. from the root of heir.]
> Inheritance; an estate that passes from an ancestor to an heir by descent or course of law; that which is inherited.

> Identify the "estate" passed from Mr. Webster to you from his investment of sixty years of life in educating the future generations.

Webster—Citizen Patriot

Noah Webster was just a young college student when the American Revolution began. He joined his father and brother in one brief skirmish of the war, reporting that he suffered more from the discomfort of mosquitoes than from bullets.

When George Washington was made Commander in Chief of the American armies, Noah Webster led a small parade of Yale students in honor of his arrival in New Haven. From this time forward Noah Webster's love and admiration for George Washington, the "Father of his country," continued to grow. A mutual friendship between these two men continued through the years and Noah Webster often stopped off at Mount Vernon on his many travels throughout the thirteen colonies.

Noah Webster was one of the first to propose a national constitution and he carried his *Sketches of American Policy* in person to Washington for study. When, in 1787, the Constitutional Convention began in Philadelphia, Noah Webster was employed there in a teaching position. The young twenty-nine year-old teacher received a stream of important visitors to his quarters, among them George Washington and Benjamin Franklin.

PAT´RIOT, n. [Fr. patriote, from L. patria, one's native country, from pater, father.]
A person who loves his country, and zealously supports and defends it and its interests.

Why can Noah Webster be called a citizen patriot?

Founding Father of American Scholarship

In the years between the end of the American Revolution and the writing of the American Constitution, Noah Webster graduated from college. With only a few gold dollars for his fortune he began to cultivate and put to work his talents for the glory of God and the good of the country.

To support himself while he was "reading law" to become a lawyer, he taught school, began research on the American language, and pondered and wrote on the subject of American government and history. He, like many of those men whom we designate as "Founding Fathers," recognized that the success of the American Christian philosophy of government would depend upon the quality of education of each individual in our republic. But unlike today, Noah Webster put the responsibility for education upon the family first and upon the individual.

Was Mr. Webster's view of education Biblical? What does the Bible say about the responsibility for education? (see Deuteronomy 6:4-9 and II Timothy 3:16)

A View of the Buildings of Yale College at New Haven

Mount Vernon, home of George Washington

SELF-TEACHING

Independence was a basic quality of the American character and Noah Webster began to write textbooks that were *self-teaching*, that is, they did not require a teacher. Through his "Spellers," "Grammars," "Readers," "Histories," any American could teach himself how to spell and write and learn the rudiments of American history and Constitutional government.

It is good to remember that early American education never depended upon the existence of schools. Most of the enterprising Americans who built America were self-educated. They learned the Bible and then they related Biblical principles to every field. While schools and colleges were established from the time of our first settlements, they primarily continued an education already commenced in every home. Education in our colonial period was a lifetime pursuit; it was education in depth.

In what ways did early education in America differ from today? Complete the T chart in your notebook, contrasting the qualities of early education in America with education today.

Early education in America	Education generally in America today
1. Self-teaching	1. Dependent upon teachers
2.	2.
3.	3.
4.	4.
5.	5.

Would you say that the outcome of colonial education was different from today? How?

What is "education in depth?"

**EVERY MAN RECEIVES TWO KINDS OF EDUCATION:
THE ONE GIVEN HIM BY SOMEONE ELSE, AND THE OTHER FAR
MORE IMPORTANT, WHICH HE GIVES HIMSELF.**

Literacy and Christianity

As one studies the history of Christianity moving westward—Christian History—one is struck by the marvelous way in which God raises up individuals and nations to advance His cause of Christ.

Noah Webster's Master's Thesis from Yale College was entitled: *Dissertation upon the Universal diffusion of Literature, as introductory to the universal diffusion of Christianity.* Literature here refers to education or "learning, skill in letters." Noah Webster believed that "the English language is to be the instrument of propagating sciences, arts, and the Christian religion to an extent probably exceeding that of any other language."

It is therefore important that the principles of English should be adjusted, and uniformity of spelling and pronunciation established and preserved, "as far as the nature of a living language will admit." This conviction that the American language was a natural bond of unity among the people of the thirteen diverse and different colonies, now states, produced America's most popular textbook—Noah Webster's "blue-backed speller." "A national language is a band of national union," wrote Noah Webster.

Explain Mr. Webster's conviction about English that inspired his "Blue-Backed Speller?"

Do you think it is just as important today to have English as a "band of national union?"

The American Spelling Book

In 1783—the year of the peace treaty that ended the American Revolution—*The American Spelling Book* was published. This book did more for American education than any other single book with the exception of the holy Bible. It was a declaration of independence from European ideas of education and it provided the principles for spelling, pronunciation, and grammar to be learned in school or out of school.

No one has been able to absolutely determine how many editions of this book were published in the 185 years since it first appeared. But it has been estimated that more than 100 million copies were sold in the first 100 years—and it is still in print today and many private schools and individuals use it. No single textbook has ever approached that record of sales.

What two books formed American education and thus the Republic?

The "Blue-Backed Speller"—so called because of its blue cover—became part of our American heritage of independence, enterprise, and energy. As our frontiers expanded, men and women carried the little fourteen-cent speller with them. It traveled with the holy Bible and enabled Americans to teach their children no matter how far they were from towns and cities. The "blue-backed speller" might be found in log cabins, on flatboats traveling the rivers and canals and on the prairie schooners—the covered wagons creaking west.

And with the spelling lessons were many short stories teaching moral precepts, many Biblical admonitions, and examples of Christian character. Some editions contained a moral catechism and character traits such as humility, mercy, peace making, purity of heart, etc. It also contained in some of its editions a short question and answer section on the United States Constitution. Many other textbooks followed Noah Webster's speller so that the fundamental subjects were covered: reading, spelling, pronunciation, grammar, American history, geography, and literature. Americans of those days who studied Noah Webster's books knew why America was the most important nation to be founded since the Christian era began.

Discuss the ways the "Blue-Backed Speller" became part of our American heritage of independence, enterprise, and energy.

American Dictionary of the English Language

Noah Webster spent sixty years of his life writing books to help his country grow up in her independence. He knew the importance of character and conscience. After some twenty-six years of work Noah Webster published his famous *An American Dictionary of the English Language*, in 1828. This book could be called the only Christian dictionary in the world, and it became the authority for the entire English-speaking world. But the final achievement in Noah Webster's plan for American Christian education was the translation of the holy Bible from its original languages. Noah Webster had learned more than twenty-eight different languages when he was working on the *American Dictionary*. Most important of these languages were those that unlocked the holy Bible. Now finally in "the most important enterprise of my life" he published an "American scriptures" for the daily reading of Americans "correctly translated into their own language."

Imagine the great task of writing the dictionary and all it required of Noah Webster.

While Mr. Webster is best known for his dictionary, what does he name the "most important enterprise of my life?" Why?

"**Education is useless without the Bible**" proclaimed Noah Webster. We have chosen to introduce you to your Christian History of America through the words of the American who established America's independence in the field of education. Like the earlier generations of Pilgrims and Puritans, Cavaliers and Friends, he believed that the holy Bible must be the basis not only of our education but the basis for all our Republican institutions. Today American education has sadly slipped away from her moorings to that great anchor—the Christian religion as defined in the holy Scriptures. The American Christian plan of education established by Noah Webster is still our heritage today.

What does it mean that the Bible is the basis for "all our Republican institutions"?

If that is true, what is the best way to restore the American Republic?

PROFI´´CIENCY, n. [from L. proficiens. from proficio, to advance forward; pro and facio, to make.] Advance in the acquisition of any art, science or knowledge; improvement; progression in knowledge.

Proficiency in Fundamental Literacy

Once again, in the tradition of American independence, it is up to the individual. It is up to you and to me. Individually each one of us can reclaim our heritage. Each one of us can become independent of ignorance, of inertia, and of irresponsibility. If we now qualify ourselves and become proficient in all of the fundamentals of education—<u>reading efficiently</u>, <u>speaking fluently and effectively</u>, and . . . <u>knowing thoroughly our American Christian history</u>, then God will truly use us and the talents which he has put into our safe-keeping so that we might glorify His name once again in America—so that her beacon light might once again be rekindled and the light of Christian liberty beam out to all the world.

Discuss how the "three I's" undermine our independence. What proficiency does Mr. Webster advise? Define proficient.

Name the three "fundamentals of education" essential to Christian liberty. Set your goal to be truly proficient in each one.

> **DO YOUR BEST TO PRESENT YOURSELF TO GOD AS ONE APPROVED, A WORKER WHO HAS NO NEED TO BE ASHAMED, RIGHTLY HANDLING THE WORD OF TRUTH.** 2 TIMOTHY 2:15

> **...AND HOW FROM CHILDHOOD YOU HAVE BEEN ACQUAINTED WITH THE SACRED WRITINGS, WHICH ARE ABLE TO MAKE YOU WISE FOR SALVATION THROUGH FAITH IN CHRIST JESUS.**
> 2 TIMOTHY 3:15

To be truly independent and proficient as you progress through your education into a fulfilling life, you will cultivate a vision for the future that employs your unique purpose in God's providence indicated by your natural interests, gifts and talents, and your heart to reach your fullest expression in Christ. Think carefully and write a three-paragraph essay that includes (1) your duty to God, (2) your thoughts of your future service, (3) and reasonable goals that would take you there.

A Word About Primary Sources

In our study, we will look to those who were the original nation makers who carried the "idea of America" in their own words. Such writings are called "primary sources" as they are the authentic accounts told fresh or originally. Secondary sources are also used—the writing of those who lived close to the historic event or in the era of study.

The style of writing and speaking, even the vocabulary used, will often sound difficult and different to our ears. Because it is important to discuss each excerpt to get the full value, the course allows ample time to discuss, debate, question, form conclusions, and record the essence of the study for future reference.

Several study helps are used:

- The Memory Tree—a diagram of an idea (example page 9)
- Primary and secondary sources within the text are shaded to set apart for identification
- Response by chatting, reflecting in writing—identified by icons
- Holding the whole "idea of America" in view by recurring diagram of overview
- Essay—digesting the idea and re-presenting it
- Maps, T-charts, summary sentences, definition

Many readings are taken from two particular compilations of primary and secondary sources. To avoid repetition, the excerpts will be abbreviated as follows with the page numbers in the two volumes:

- *CHOC* – *The Christian History of the Constitution of the United States: Christian Self-Government*, V.M. Hall.
- *T&L* – *Teaching and Learning America's Christian History: the Principle Approach*, R.J. Slater

    All definitions are taken from *American Dictionary of the English Language*, Noah Webster, 1828.

    In the excerpts from these publications, emphasis is indicated for the benefit of the student.

Character Forms a Free or a Fettered Life
The Individual Character and How Men are Governed

FET´TERED, pp. Bound or confined by fetters; enchained.

Education forms character — Character forms a free or a fettered life — Individual responsibility, duty and standards

What is character? The memory tree above diagrams the major points of how character forms a free or a fettered life. First let's define character with Mr. Webster:

CHAR'ACTER, n. A mark made by cutting or engraving . . . The peculiar qualities, impressed by nature or habit on a person, which distinguish him from others.

This definition implies that character is "cut" or "engraved" – formed, forged, and structured by "nature or habit". Therefore an instrument is required to do the forming. That instrument might be family, church, and most certainly schooling.

Then what is Christian character? Is it not an individual character that is formed, forged, and structured by Christ and that reflects His character?

Discuss and memorize the definition as diagrammed:

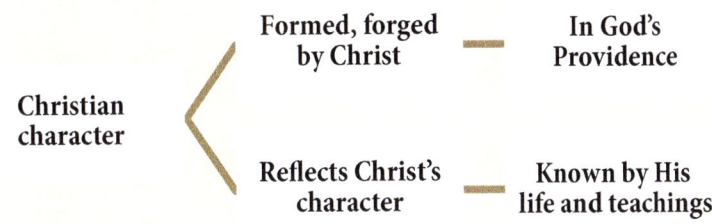

Record the diagram of the Christian character definition. Do you recognize the ways your character is being formed? List the aspects of Christian character being formed in you.

Individual Responsibilities

The following pages quote selections taken from "Letters to a Young Gentleman Commencing His Education" by Noah Webster, Esq., 1823, as the context of the discussion of individual responsibilities and duty and standards of behavior.[1]

HINTS FOR FUTURE HAPPINESS

"As you are now commencing a course of classical education, and need the guidance of those who have preceded you in the same course, you cannot but receive with kindness, and treat with attention, the remarks of a friend, whose affection for you, excites in him a deep solicitude for your future reputation and happiness. I feel the more desirous to furnish you with some hints for the direction of your studies, for I have experienced the want of such helps myself; no small portions of my life having been spent in correcting the errors of my early education.

 How does correct guidance benefit a young life?

IMITATION AS AN INFLUENCE OF CHARACTER

"It has been often remarked, that men are the creatures of habit. The rudiments of knowledge we receive by tradition; and our first actions are, in a good degree, modeled by imitation. Nor ought it to be otherwise. The respect which young persons feel for their parents, superiors and predecessors is no less the dictate of reason, than the requirement of heaven; and the propensity to imitation, is no less natural, than it may be useful. These principles however, like many others, when pursued or indulged to an extreme, produce evil effects; as they often lead the young to embrace error as well as truth.

 What are the benefits and dangers of imitation in a young life?

STAGES OF LIFE

"Some degree of confidence in the opinions of those whom we respect, is always a duty—"

- In the first stages of life, our confidence in parents must be implicit—and our obedience to their will, complete and unreserved.
- In later stages of life, as the intellectual faculties expand and the reasoning power gains strength, implicit confidence in the opinions even of the most distinguished men, ceases to be a duty.
- How does one judge the opinions of others?
    - We are to regard their opinions only as probably correct;
    - But refer the ultimate decision of this point to evidence to be collected from our own reasoning or researches.
    - All men are liable to err; and knowledge of this fact should excite in us constant solicitude to obtain satisfactory reasons for every opinion we embrace.

 How does duty differ in various stages of life? How does one judge opinions in later life?

---

1 Noah Webster, *Letters to a Young Gentleman Commencing His Education: Letter I* (New Haven: Howe & Spalding, 1823), 5-20.

Individual Duties

💬 *Ponder and discuss the definitions of reason and revelation to fully understand Webster's guidance:*

> REASON, n. re'zn. *A faculty of the mind by which it distinguishes truth from falsehood, and good from evil, and which enables the possessor to deduce inferences from facts or from propositions.*
>
> REVELA'TION, n. *[Fr. from L. revelatus, revelo. See Reveal.] the sacred truths which God has communicated to man for his instruction and direction. (the Bible)*

✎ *Describe reason, the factor that makes humans human, in your own words. Is it natural to all people? What gives some people the power to reason well? What difference does it make?*

"Reason Without Revelation is a Miserable Guide"

"As men are furnished with powers of reason, it is obviously the design of the creator, that reason should be employed as their guide, in every stage of life. But reason, without cultivation, without experience and without the aids of revelation, is a miserable guide; it often errs from ignorance, and more often from the impulse of passion. The first questions a rational being should ask himself, are: Who made me? Why was I made? What is my duty?

"The proper answers to these questions, and the practical results, constitute, my dear friend, the whole business of life."

💬 *Explain "reason without revelation" and how it "errs." What are the questions that constitute the "whole business of life?"*

"**Now reason, unaided by revelation, cannot answer these questions.** The experience of the pagan world has long since determined this point. Revelation alone furnishes satisfactory information on these subjects. Let it then be the first study that occupies your mind, to learn from the scriptures the character and will of your maker; the end or purpose for which he gave you being and intellectual powers, and the duties he requires you to perform. In all that regards faith and practice, the scriptures furnish the principles, precepts and rules, by which you are to be guided. Your reputation among men; your own tranquility of mind in this life; and all rational hope of future happiness, depend on an exact conformity of conduct to the commands of God revealed in the sacred oracles."

✎ *Ponder the three questions Mr. Webster suggests are vital to every life and actually constitute the "whole business of life." How would you answer each question with Webster's advice in mind? Who made me? Why was I made? What is my duty?*

Why is revelation necessary to reason? What does your reputation, your peace, and your happiness depend upon?

💬 *Could a complete philosophy of life be based upon Mr. Webster's guidance?*

The Nature of Things: Natural Law

Washington refusing a dictatorship

Law is basic to nature and therefore to life. Mr. Ben Gilmore, a master teacher of American government and Christian history explains the "nature of things." Listen carefully as he explains how to "reason" about the nature of life:

I know of only three human organizations that God created in the Bible: (1) Family, (2) Church, and (3) State. The family is the building block of every society, Christian and non-Christian. Every society has a vertical relationship with some sort of higher power. We call that vertical relationship between families and God (or a god) Church. We call the horizontal relationship between families and families State.

Jesus Christ was asked about the most important commandment. "And he answering said, 'Thou shalt love the Lord thy God with all thy heart, and with all thy soul, and with all thy strength, and with all thy mind; and thy neighbor as thyself." [Luke 10:27]. Again there exists the vertical and the horizontal relationship. Throughout human history the quality of the vertical relationship in a society has always determined the quality of the horizontal relationship. Never the other way around. This holds true in families, churches and civil governments.

The family, the church, and the state are governmental organizations. This means that they need direction, regulation, control, and restraint. The best set of rules by which to govern families, churches, and civil governments are found in the Bible.

But what rules governed before the Bible? They are called, "The laws of nature." Things were "good" or "bad" long before the books of the Bible were written. Further – something is not good or bad just because the Bible says so. The Bible says something is good or bad because *it has always been so.*

The founding fathers understood that, when they referred to "the laws of Nature and of Nature's God" in our Declaration of Independence. The laws of nature are called, <u>Natural Law</u>. The laws of nature's God are called, <u>Revealed Law</u> and are found only in the Holy Scriptures.

Natural laws are discovered by observation and reason. (Sometimes children learn not to touch a hot stove by touching one.) Revealed law is learned by study and prayer. Natural and Revealed Law will never be in conflict because they were both created by God. However, Revealed Law is infinitely more authoritative than Natural Law. Revealed law was "dictated" by revelation by God. Natural Law is discovered by human observation and human reason, both of which are imperfect.

Natural Law predated Revealed Law by thousands of years. Sir William Blackstone speculated that because man had neglected to reason it out, God in His benevolence gave us the Bible to help us understand how to love Him and love one another.

It is so simple it becomes profound – Our whole purpose is to learn to love God and to love one another. God even took the form of a man, Jesus Christ, to demonstrate how it is done. Then He came again as the Holy Spirit to guide us.

Think about it. The infinite first cause of everything wants to teach you to love Him and others. He has done and continues doing everything possible, short of violating your will, to get your attention.

How would you summarize Mr. Gilmore's explanation of "the nature of things?" Can you explain how law is the "Nature of things"?

Natural law is codified in the Ten Commandments in the revealed law.

The Ten Commandments and the Two Great Commandments

"**The duties of men are summarily comprised in the Ten Commandments,** consisting of two tables. One table comprehends the duties that we owe immediately to God—the other, the duties we owe to our fellow men. Christ himself has reduced these commandments under two general precepts, which enjoin upon us to love the Lord our God with all our heart, with all our soul, with all our mind and with all our strength—and to love our neighbor as ourselves. On these Two Great Commandments hang all the law and the prophets—that is, they comprehend the substance of all the doctrines and precepts of the Bible, or the whole of religion."

Discuss the commandments that comprise your duty to God. Then discuss the commandments that comprise our duty to each other. Can you think of anything Jesus taught that does not fall under one of the Ten Commandments? Or under the two Great Commandments?

The Ten Commandments and the Two

At the end of this section you will complete the chart with the standards that relate to each commandment.

The Ten Commandments are something so familiar to us in many ways but also removed from our daily thinking. Most of us think of it as the list of "do nots" from God. The reality is that the Ten Commandments are so much more than that. They are the keys to a good life. They are the keys to your happiness. In addition to the ten, God gave two great commandments which are to "love the Lord your God with all your heart, your soul, your mind and your strength" and "to love your neighbor as yourself." These two directly correspond to the two tables of the Ten Commandments: the first table or Commandments I-V show us how to love the LORD, and the second table or Commandments VI-X show us how to love our neighbor. Understood in this way, the Ten Commmandments are really a set of loving rules which teach us how to love the LORD and love our neighbor. The Ten Commandments are our moral code teaching us how to live free and happy. [2]

Dennis Prager, in his *The Ten Commandments: Still the Best Moral Code*,[3] gives an excellent, simple and direct commentary that presents the following understanding:

I. God wants us to be free! "I am the Lord Your God who took you out of Egypt."

II. No other Gods! Eliminate false gods; worship the God of the Ten Commandments to make a good world.

III. Do not misuse God's name! God is good; do not call evil good.

IV. Remember the Sabbath! Don't be a slave; honor the Sabbath as it brings you faith in God.

V. Honor your Father and Mother! It is fundamental to society for survival.

VI. Do not Murder! Protect human life.

VII. Do not commit adultery! Honor family; adultery destroys it.

VIII. Do not steal! Protect the sanctity of people's property by not stealing a life, a person, a spouse, material property, intellectual property, a reputation, dignity, or trust.

IX. Do not bear false witness! Lying is the root of all evil; there is no cause more important than telling the truth.

X. Do not covet! Do not seek to take away and own something that belongs to another person as it leads to evil.

---

[2] Rebecca H. Beach, "*The Goodness and the Liberty of the Two and the Ten*," 2016, MS, Sacramento.
[3] Dennis Prager, *The Ten Commandments: Still the Best Moral Code* (Regnery Publishing, 2015).

Christian Self-Government

> "Have you ever thought of what the subject of "government" means to you as an American Christian? Most of us think of the subject of "government" as *external* to us, that is, located at the seat of civil government in the state or national capital. With the establishment of America as a Christian nation we restored the original Scriptural concept of government as stemming from God's control of the individual because that individual accepted and acknowledged the sovereignty of God through Jesus Christ."

> GŎV´ERNMENT, n. Direction; regulation. 2. Control; restraint. Men are apt to neglect the government of their temper and passions. 3. The exercise of authority; direction and restraint exercised over the actions of men in communities, societies or states; the administration of public affairs, according to established constitution, laws and usages, or by arbitrary edicts.

Think of the nations you may know that operate by a pagan system of government presently or historically. What do you know about those nations and the state of their people?

The success of American Christian Constitutional Government depends upon this principle of Christian self-government. But this principle cannot operate successfully unless lives are obedient to God's government of them. We can begin with the Commandments of the Lord given to us in his written Word. Much more responsibility is required on our part to give conscious attention to the fulfillment of God's law in our lives.

Is more personal responsibility required to maintain liberty in a system of self-government than in a pagan system? Why and what is the alternative?

Self-government involves some limitation of the individual. What is the difference between self-limitation and external limitation imposed by a pagan government?

Explain which system you would choose if you were given the choice and why?

Living by Standards

Noah Webster is now going to give some time and attention as to how the Commandments are related to everything that one does in daily life—in other words, a discussion of the standards of conduct based upon the Ten Commandments.

> Standard, n. That which is established by sovereign power as a rule or measure by which others are to be adjusted.

Record the definition of standard. Discuss how living by standards protects you and others and brings blessing to all. As you study the following discussion of standards to live by, decide and name the commandment upon which each standard rests.

Delighting in Moral Excellence

"The first duty of man then is to love and reverence the Supreme Being. The fear of God is the beginning of wisdom or religion. But the love of God implies some knowledge of his character and attributes—and these are to be learned partly by a view of his stupendous works in creation, but chiefly from the revelations of himself recorded in the Scriptures.

"The great constituent of love to the Supreme Being is however an entire complacency [pleasure] in his character and attributes, and unqualified approbation [consent] to his law, as a rule of life. Such complacency [pleasure] and approbation [consent] can exist only in a holy heart—a heart that delights in moral excellence. But wherever they exist, they produce a correspondent purity of life.

"The natural effect then of <u>a real conformity of *heart*</u> to the First and Great Commandment, which enjoins supreme love to God, is, to produce conformity of life to the injunction of the second command, to love our neighbor as ourselves."

Commandment _____

Write and discuss the definition of 'delight'

DELI´GHT, v. t. [Sp. *deleytar*; Port. *deleitar*; L. *delector*; Fr. *delecter*] 1. To affect with great pleasure; to please highly; to give or afford high satisfaction or joy. *I will delight myself in thy statutes. Ps. 119.*

Create a T-chart of reasons we have to delight in God:

Who God Is	What God Does

Full Meaning of the Commandments

"In applying the commands of God to practice, be careful to give to them the full intended latitude of meaning. The love of God comprehends the love of all his attributes—the love of his *justice* in condemning and punishing sin—as well as of his *mercy* in forgiving and saving penitent sinners—the love of his *sovereignty* as well as of his *grace*.

The divine character is an entire thing—and there can be no genuine love to the Supreme Being that does not embrace his whole character. When in obedience to the third Commandment of the Decalogue, you would avoid profane swearing, you are to remember that this alone is not a full compliance with the prohibition, which comprehends all irreverent words or actions and whatever tends to cast contempt on the Supreme Being, or on his word and ordinances."

Commandment _____

💬 *Do we selectively appreciate God's character as our individual behavior makes it convenient? What does it mean to embrace His whole character?*

Respecting Parents

"The command to honor your father and mother comprehends not only due respect and obedience to your parents; but all due respect to other superiors. The distinction of age, is one established by God himself, and is perhaps the only difference of rank in society, which is of divine origin. It is a distinction of the utmost importance to society, it cannot be destroyed, and it ought not to be forgotten. Hence filial respect has ever been esteemed one of the most amiable virtues.

Let your respect for your parents, and others who are of like age or standing in society, be sincere, cordial and uniform; and let the feelings of your heart be manifest in your exterior deportment. Never forget the <u>deference</u> due to their age, nor treat them with a familiarity that is incompatible with that deference. Even the customary forms of address should not be overlooked, or neglected; for in doing honor to age, you honor a divine command, and secure to yourself a source of permanent consolation. It will afford you particular satisfaction, when your parents are consigned to the tomb."

Commandment _____

✍ *Record the definitions in your notebook and rephrase in your own words:*

📖 Respect, n. That estimation or honor in which men hold the distinguished worth or substantial good qualities of others.

Deference, n. A yielding in opinion; submission of judgment to the opinion or judgment of another. Hence, regard; respect.

💬 *What is the blessing promised by the fifth commandment?*

Property

"From your education and principles, it is presumed that there is little need of cautioning you against a violation of the eighth commandment, by a felonious taking of the property of another, in a manner to incur the penalties of human laws. But the prohibition covers much broader ground—<u>it extends to every species of fraud or deception by which the property of another is taken or withheld from him.</u>

"If in receiving or paying money, a mistake throws into your hands a sum of money beyond what is your right, it is a violation of the eighth command to retain that sum in your own hands, let it be never so small. You are under the same moral obligation to return the surplus money to the rightful owner, as you are not to take a like sum from him by theft."

"Be very careful then to resist every temptation to deception and fraud. Let every transaction with your fellow men be just and honorable. This is required no less by your own reputation, than by the law of God; *for deception* in every form is meanness."

"Nor would I have you more careful of your neighbor's property than of his good name, which is dearer to him than his property. Say nothing of your neighbor falsely; and never publish his faults unless to circumscribe their influence, or prevent an injury to other men."

Commandment _____

Webster gives some examples of honoring the principle of property as expressed in the eighth commandment. Discuss each of the following and determine how it relates to the revealed law:

- "In like manner, in trade, the man who by deception, gets a dollar more for an article than the purchaser would have given, had he not been deceived, is in view of God, as guilty as if he had taken that dollar from the purchaser's chest.

- "The man who by an artifice conceals the defects of his goods, or gives them a false appearance, and thus deceives the purchaser, is guilty of fraud; and any money that he may get by this deception is taken as wrongfully as if taken by theft.

- "The farmer who brings his produce to market, and sells it in a bad state, knowing it to be defective and concealing the defect, or giving a false representation of it, is guilty of fraud and falls within the purview of the eighth command.

- "The man who adulterates his drugs, and sells them as genuine, certainly violates the eighth command, and may violate the sixth.

- "The wine seller and the distiller who mix and adulterate their liquors, and sell them for what they are not, are guilty of fraud, and in a greater or less degree, fall within the prohibition of the eighth command; and by using poisonous substances in such adulteration, they may incur the guilt of the sixth.

- "The methods by which this command is violated in the ordinary commerce of life are literally innumerable – and if judgment should be laid to the line, who could stand?

- "Be very careful then to resist every temptation to deception and fraud. Let every transaction with your fellow men be just and honorable. This is required no less by our own reputation than by the law of God; for deception in every form is meanness.

- "Nor would I have you more careful of your neighbor's property than of his good name, which is dearer to him than his property. Say nothing of your neighbor falsely; and never publish his faults unless to circumscribe their influence, or prevent an injury to other men."

Real Worth or Dignity of Character

"Let it then be the first study of your early years, to learn in what consists *real worth or dignity of character*. To ascertain this important point, consider the character and attributes of the Supreme Being. As God is the only perfect Being in the Universe, his character, consisting of all that is good and great, must be the model of all human excellence; and his laws must of course be the only rules of conduct by which his rational creatures can reach any portion of like excellence. In the very nature of things then a man is exalted in proportion to his conformity to the divine standard of worth; and degraded in proportion to his want of conformity to that standard."

 RECTITUDE, n. In morality, rightness of principle or practice; uprightness of mind; exact conformity to truth, or to the rules prescribed for moral conduct, either by divine or human laws. Rectitude of mind is the disposition to act in conformity to any known standard of right, truth or justice; rectitude of conduct is the actual conformity to such standard. Perfect rectitude belongs only to the Supreme Being. The more nearly the rectitude of men approaches to the standard of the divine law, the more exalted and dignified is their character. Want of rectitude is not only sinful, but debasing.

💬 *What is the meaning of 'exalted'; 'debasing'?*

> "Nothing can be *really honorable* and *dignified* which is not in *exact accordance with* rectitude. Let this be imprinted on your mind as the first principle of moral science. A violation of human laws implies *meanness* as well as *wickedness*; it impairs the reputation and lessens the moral worth of the offender—much more does a transgression of the Divine Law, imply want of dignity and self-respect as well as contempt for the Supreme Lawgiver—it sinks a man in his own estimation and debases him in the opinion of his fellow-men."
>
> Commandment _____

💬 *Discuss the definition of rectitude.*

✍ *Paraphrase the definition of rectitude.*

Real Honor

> "Nothing can be more false than the opinion that *honor* can exist without *moral rectitude*. Every violation of moral duty is *meanness* as well as *crime*—for it implies a disposition to offend or treat with contempt the greatest and best Being in the Universe, or a disposition to injure a fellow citizen, or both: and a disposition in one being to injure another, implies a want of that benevolence and love of justice which are essential to greatness of mind, which regards primarily the common welfare and happiness of moral beings.
>
> "Real honor then consists in a disposition to promote the best interests of the human family—that is, in an exact conformity of heart and life to the divine precepts. Whatever voluntary conduct in man impairs human happiness or introduces disorder into society manifests a defect of character, destitution of honorable principles.
>
> Commandment _____

📖 HON´OR, n. on´or. [L. honor, honos; Fr. honneur; Sp. honor; Port. honra; It. onore; Arm. enor; Ir. onoir.] The esteem due or paid to worth; high estimation.

💬 *Discuss the definition of HONOR.*

Dealing with Offenses

📖 Dueling (definition) "The fighting of two persons one against the other, at an appointed time and place, upon a precedent quarrel." [*The American and English Encyclopedia of Law*, 1888] Dueling is now forbidden by law in America. In what other ways do people endeavor to get satisfaction when someone has offended them?

What is the Christian approach to this whole problem on the giving or receiving of "offense?"

📖 OFFENSE, n. offens´ 1. Displeasure; anger, or moderate anger. He gave them just cause of offense. He took offense. 3. Any transgression of law, divine or human; a crime; sin; act of wickedness or omission of duty.

💬 *Discuss the definition of the word offense. What is the Biblical standard of dealing with offenses?*

"On the subject of dueling, I would farther observe, that the practice, far from exhibiting unequivocal proof of true courage, evinces, in my view, the most disgraceful cowardice. It proves a man to be more afraid of the scorn of perverted minds, than of the wrath of heaven, or the vengeance of the law—more afraid of incurring the contempt of unprincipled men, than of forfeiting the favor of the most perfect judge of right and wrong, and of the most virtuous of his fellow-citizens—more afraid of a temporary stigma on his own reputation, than of sacrificing all his obligations to his family and friends, and of plunging his parents, his wife, his children, and his brethren in the deepest distress—nay, if married, more afraid of popular odium incurred by manly rectitude, than of violating his solemn marriage vows, which have pledged his veracity and his honor, to provide for his consort, and to cherish her with tenderness. This species of cowardice, this miserable, this mean obsequiousness to popular prejudice, is evidence of a degraded mind, and an indelible stain on the human character.

💬 *Discuss the meaning of 'more afraid of the scorn of perverted minds . . .' and "obsequiousness to . . . "*

"There is another view of this subject which ought not to be overlooked. Duels almost always originate in a defect of true politeness—and a challenge accepted is presumptive evidence that the parties are *not* gentlemen, in the sense in which the word should always be understood, and in which alone it can *be correctly* used. A real gentleman never voluntarily gives offense; and if he offends without design, he instantly acknowledges his error. The offended party, if a real gentleman, will as promptly accept this acknowledgment.

💬 *What is Webster's mark of a real gentleman?*

"If the parties differ as to the nature and aggravation of the offense, and the value of the atonement offered, if they are really gentlemen, they will readily submit the decision of the question to an impartial friend, and rest satisfied with his decision. In nine cases of ten, perhaps in every case of an appeal to arms, to obtain satisfaction for injuries or affronts, it may be clearly seen by the impartial world that the affair has proceeded from a defect of *real honor* and *good breeding* in one party or in both. Instead therefore of vindicating their honor by arms, they manifest to the world that they are destitute of the genuine principles of good breeding, and of the real magnanimity which is characteristic of gentlemen."

Commandment _____

"A Lonely Duel" by Howard Pyle

Part I: America's Heritage of Christian Character

📝 *Because we are all capable of giving and receiving offenses, Matthew 18:15-17 gives specific counsel about resolving offenses. What is the Christian approach to this whole problem on the giving or receiving of "offense?"*

Write a brief description of the method of resolving offenses suggested.

Furnishing the Mental House:
"Conscience Is The Most Sacred Of All Property."

"In selecting books for reading, be careful to choose such as furnish the best helps to improvement in morals, literature, arts and science; preferring profit to pleasure, and instruction to amusement. A small portion of time may be devoted to such reading as tends to relax the mind, and to such bodily amusements as serve to invigorate muscular strength and the vital functions. But the greatest part of life is to be employed in useful labors, and in various indispensable duties, private, social and public.

"Man has but little time to spare for the gratification of the senses and the imagination. I would therefore caution you against the fascinations of plays, novels, romances, and that species of descriptive writing which is employed to embellish common objects, without much enlarging the bounds of knowledge, or to paint imaginary scenes, which only excite curiosity, and a temporary interest; and then vanish in empty air. "The readers of books may be comprehended in two classes—those who read chiefly for amusement, and those who read for instruction. The first, and far the most numerous class, give their money and their time for private gratification; the second employ both for the acquisition of knowledge, which they expect to apply to some useful purpose. The first, gain subjects of conversation and social entertainment; the second, acquire the means of public usefulness, and of private elevation of character."

Commandment _____

💬 *Have you ever thought of comparing what you read—books, magazines, etc. with "food?" Books especially can be described as "food" for the mind and the heart. So it is well to consider what one's mind is "eating" and what one's heart is set upon. Think of your mind as a "mental house" in which you live. How would you furnish it to give you the food you need to fulfill your God-given purpose in life?*

Friendship

"In forming your connections in society, be careful to select for your companions, young men [friends] of good breeding, and of virtuous principles and habits. The company of the profligate and irreligious is to be shunned as poison. You cannot always avoid some intercourse [connections] with men of dissolute lives; but you can always select, for your intimate associates, men of good principles and unimpeachable character. Never maintain a familiar connection with the profane, the lewd, the intemperate, the gamester, or the scoffer at religion. Towards men of such character, the common civilities of life are to be observed—beyond these, nothing is required of men who reverence the divine precepts, and who desire, to 'keep themselves unspotted from the world.'"

Commandment _____

✎ *Friendships are important and even vital to a full life. Find the Christian standard for friendships in the Bible. (Proverbs 22:11; Proverbs 27:9; Proverbs 17:17; Proverbs 22:24) Make a list of the individual qualities of worthy friendships. What kinds of character should be avoided?*

"A Republican Form of Government

is evidently the most rational form that men have devised for the protection of person and property, and for securing liberty. But hitherto no means have been devised to guard this form of government from abuse and corruption. Men in republics are as wicked, and as selfish as in monarchies, and with far more power to introduce disorders, both into legislation and into the administration of the laws. In republics, the influence of selfish and ambitious men over the weak, the ignorant and unsuspecting, has its full range of operation; and sooner or later, this influence will place in office incompetent men, or men who will sacrifice principle to personal emolument or aggrandizement. The corruption of the electors is the first step towards the ruin of republics; and when the sources of power are corrupted, the evil hardly admits of a remedy."

Commandment _____

✎ *Why is Christian character necessary, even essential, in a republic?*

💬 *Why is it important to scrutinize a man's campaign practices—the ways and means by which men seek promotion to public office?*

Personal Conduct in School

"In the prosecution of your studies, endeavor to make yourself master of whatever you attempt to learn. Understand well the rudiments or first principles of every branch of study, whether in literature or in science. The first principles are often difficult to beginners; but when you have overcome the first difficulties, your progress will be more easy and pleasant."

Commandment _____

…ABOVE ALL THINGS LOSE NO OCCASION OF EXERCISING YOUR DISPOSITIONS TO BE GRATEFUL, TO BE GENEROUS, TO BE CHARITABLE, TO BE HUMANE, TO BE TRUE, JUST, FIRM, ORDERLY, COURAGEOUS, ETC. CONSIDER EVERY ACT OF THIS KIND AS AN EXERCISE WHICH WILL STRENGTHEN YOUR MORAL FACULTIES, & INCREASE YOUR WORTH.

THOMAS JEFFERSON TO PETER CARR 1787

The Commandments Chart and Essay

There is a difference between an educational program based upon teaching you certain facts and ideas and one teaching you the "rudiments" or principles of every subject. What is the difference? Which system gives you the greatest opportunity for the development of your own individual talents? Why?

The Commandments Chart has a column for "Standards." Complete the chart by adding the standards Webster has discussed in the appropriate place according to the Ten Commandments.

Two Commandments	Ten Commandments	Standards of Living

ESSAY Using the memory tree below as a guide, write an essay on individual responsibility and duty as a record of Mr. Webster's good advice.

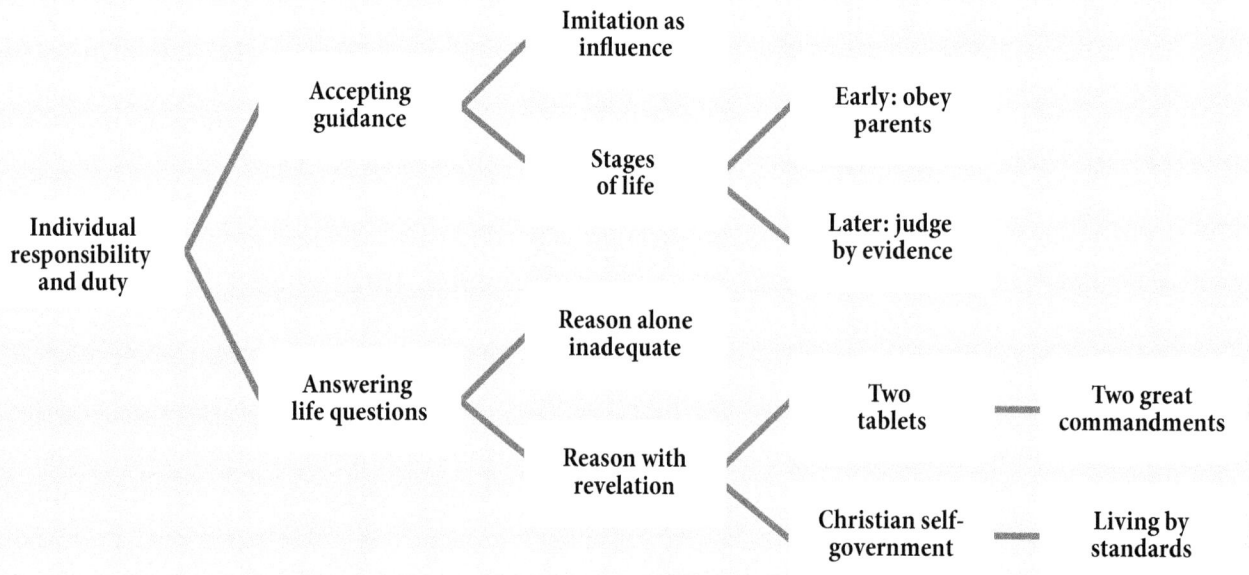

Part I: America's Heritage of Christian Character

American Education Models

Today in our nation, several models of education are practiced. The public schools employ methods that are entirely secular in nature. Private and Christian schools most often employ traditional methods of education that are more conservative but still influenced by the "progressive" methods introduced by John Dewey in the early twentieth century to instill socialistic ideals in American youth. Because we are a pluralistic society practicing religious liberty, there are other religion-based methods of education practiced.

Before we compare methods, let's look at the authentic American education model demonstrated in the education of a young man of the Revolutionary war era who later became an outstanding statesman.

American Christian Model of Education: The Principle Approach[4]

JOHN QUINCY ADAMS

The Education of John Quincy Adams: The Character for a Christian Republic by Rosalie Slater, pages 602–616 of The Christian History of the American Revolution: Consider and Ponder. *Read the essay in its entirety.*

"One of the most critical changes we have witnessed in American education has been the change away from the reasoning, writing, and reflecting ability so prominent in the generations that produced the Declaration of Independence, the Constitution of the United States of America, the Monroe Doctrine, and other documents. This ability to define a philosophy of government in writing was the result of a colonial education in principles, leading ideas, and their application to the field of civil government—America's unique contribution."

List in your notebook the sequence of formal and informal schooling that produced the character of leadership and service in the education of John Quincy Adams. Look particularly for the three elements Mr. Webster says are <u>essential to the U.S. Republic</u> and identify the evidences of the three essentials in John Quincy Adams' education.

Education is useless without the Bible	
Proficiency in fundamentals	
Thorough knowledge of history	

---

4 R.J. Slater, "The Education of John Quincy Adams: The Character for a Christian Republic" in *The Christian History of the American Revolution: Consider and Ponder* (FACE, 1976), 602-616.

ESSAY *How does John Quincy Adams' life illustrate the two principles: 1) Education forms character, and 2) Character forms a free or a fettered life?*

Other Views of God and Man

From the beginning of time there have been views of God and man opposed to natural and revealed law. Unreasonable as it may seem to be in conflict with the laws of the universe, rebellion began with Lucifer and has persisted defeat after defeat through the ages. It is wise to capture the essence (principles) of opposing views to ensure wise counsel and discerning judgment.

A comparison of the Christian view of God and man to a secular view of God and man presents clear contrasts easily seen *(secular: pertaining to this present world, or to things not spiritual or holy)*.

Ponder and discuss the models that follow in contrast to Christianity. The chart presents the views of God and man from which can be derived a view of education. As you discuss each one, consider the quality of character each approach might form.

Christian and Secular Views of God as Basis of Education
CHRISTIANITY AND SECULARISM

View of	Christianity	Secularism
Origins	I was created by a supernatural God, the God of the Bible.	I am the product of random, unknown, impersonal, natural forces.
Source of knowledge	God reveals Himself and all knowledge to man.	Man's mind and reason alone lead him to all 'truth.'
What is good	God is of ultimate value and goodness. The purpose of life is to glorify Him.	Man is of ultimate value and goodness. Life is for man's purposes only.
Future	God has a plan for the earth and man and He is establishing His kingdom.	The earth, and physical existence, is all there is. The future is purposeless, for we are controlled by random processes.

How would you describe the quality of character that might be produced by secularism?

Christianity and Socialism

View of	Christianity	Socialism
Law	God is the lawmaker. He has revealed to us His law in nature (natural law) and the Bible (revealed law).	Law is solely a product of man, and is evolving as man evolves. Law is what those in power say it is.
Government	God created government, and He gives the principles for its operation.	**Government** is purely a human invention for the benefit of mankind. As is true of all things, it is evolving.
Man's Nature/ Control	God designed us to govern or control ourselves by His Spirit, according to His Word. Christian self-government is the ideal.	**Man** is controlled by various forces outside of himself (such as other men, his emotions, civil governments, environmental factors).
Private Property	God instituted individual, private ownership of property and voluntary exchange, without the intervention of civil government.	**Private Property** is the root of all evil. Civil government should either own or control all property. Government intervention into the economic sphere of life is beneficial.

How would you describe the quality of character that might be produced by socialism?

THE EDUCATION OF ALL CHILDREN FROM THE MOMENT THAT THEY CAN GET ALONG WITHOUT A MOTHER'S CARE, SHALL BE IN STATE INSTITUTIONS AT STATE EXPENSE.
KARL MARX

GIVE ME FOUR YEARS TO TEACH YOUR CHILDREN AND THE SEEDS I HAVE SOWN WILL NEVER BE UPROOTED ... GIVE US THE CHILD FOR 8 YEARS AND IT WILL BE A BOLSHEVIK FOREVER.
VLADIMIR LENIN

Christianity and Communism

View of	Christianity	Communism
God	The source of sovereign authority is found in God alone. The God of the Bible is sovereign over all areas of life, including politics and civil government. He created men and nations for His own glory and good purposes.	"Man makes religion, religion doesn't make man. Religion is the self-consciousness and self-esteem of man who has either not yet found himself or has already lost himself again." (Karl Marx, *The Communist Manifesto*)
Man	God created man, sustains him, offers Him the free gift of life by salvation through Christ. Man is of infinite value and is destined for immortality.	"The human being is in the most literal sense a *political animal* not merely a gregarious animal, but an animal which can individuate itself only in the midst of society." (Marx, *The Grundrisse* 1857)
Government	The purpose of civil government is explicitly stated by God as punishment of evildoers and the rewarding of those who do good. As such it is limited in its scope.	"Political power, properly so called, is merely the organized power of one class for oppressing another." (Karl Marx, *The Communist Manifesto*) The practical outworking of communist theory has been the establishment of a dictatorship as the form of government."
Property	God, the creator and Owner of all things, created man in his image; all that was made-visible and invisible-is God's property. God commanded man to be fruitful, multiply and subdue the earth and thus man has been given the duty and responsibility of dominion over and stewardship of God's creation. Private ownership of property is essential to man's freedom and well being.	"The theory of Communism may be summed up in one sentence: Abolish all private property." (Karl Marx, *The Communist Manifesto*)

How would you describe the quality of character that might be produced by communism?

Sometimes less obvious are the views of God and man of other religions. For instance, Islam is a religion we are beginning to know better as many of the conflicts in the world today are in areas dominated by Islam. While the god of Islam is Allah, it is important to realize that Allah is not the God of the Bible. The chart below compares the two views.

CHRISTIANITY AND ISLAM

View of	Christianity	Islam
God is . . .	Father	Allah is master
Man is . . .	Child	Man is submitted to Allah
The motive for worship is . . .	Love	Submission
The requirement is . . .	Obedience Hopeful – abundant life	Submission Fatalistic – longing for death

 How would you describe the quality of character that might be produced by Islam?

Emphatic Conclusion and Analysis of American Education

You now have an understanding of the role of character in your personal life and calling as well as in the life of a nation. You have seen that the standards you choose to pattern your character have far-reaching effects in forming your leadership and service. In other words, the quality of your character determines your happiness and success in life. But it also results in a life that enjoys liberty in Christ or a life enslaved to sin. The reasoning you have accomplished through your reading, discussion, and writing has given you the ability to articulate this essential idea: the necessity of Christian character to a Republic.

 To help solidify your understanding, practice presenting the idea to a classmate. This will show you how well you truly understand and if there are areas of incomplete thinking. Ask your classmate to question you at the conclusion of your presentation. Then allow your classmate to present the idea to you.

How do the four forms of American education practiced today in the United States answer the questions posed by Noah Webster: Who made me? Why was I made? What is my duty? Design a chart to record this analysis.

Part I Essay

"The Necessity of Christian Character to the American Republic and What that Means to Me"
Incorporate the major concepts of the five parts of Nation Makers in your essay.

Committee of Franklin, Jefferson, Adams, Livingston, and Sherman consulting on the Declaration of Independence

---

WE DESTROY ARGUMENTS AND EVERY LOFTY OPINION RAISED AGAINST THE KNOWLEDGE OF GOD, AND TAKE EVERY THOUGHT CAPTIVE TO OBEY CHRIST . . . II CORINTHIANS 10:5

Nation Makers
Part II:
The Blessing of Self-Government

Self-Government — Individuality — God's Hand — Links on the Chain

The Blessing of Self-Government

It is a great privilege to live in a nation where the right of self-government is acknowledged as the basis of civil government. You will see as we continue our study that self-government is at the heart of the "idea of America". Never before in history did any nation afford its people such a blessing. The story itself is your story and self-government is your stewardship.

Notice again the "Preview of *Nation Makers*" on page 10 and see that the theme "The Blessing of Self-Government" has several basic understandings:

- **God's Principle of Individuality**
- **God's Hand in Human History (Providential History)**
- **The Chain of Christianity®**

These themes constitute the "big picture" of how the blessing of self-government came about. What is the benefit to you of internalizing the "idea of America"?

Doing so enables you to maximize the liberty you have inherited as an American citizen. Then you can use the same principles of liberty to achieve the fullest expression of your individual value in Christ in your life and service.

By the end of the course you will be able to articulate the "idea of America" from your heart. What are your personal goals for your life? Think of these as you continue the study and ponder your part in the magnificent history of the "idea of America".

 Note in your notebook the theme of this chapter and its major concepts.

Christian Liberty Becomes Civil Liberty

In *Nation Makers Part I,* we witnessed the fact that God uses individual character to forward His story. Isn't it exciting and inspiring to see history from the perspective that gives value to every human life, and to see the big picture of God's greater purposes that imparts the wisdom of the ages?

First, look again at the cover of *Nation Makers*. The artist Howard Pyle brings to life dramatically the sacrifice, the strength, and the resolution that produced the first Christian Republic in the history of the world. Howard Pyle saw the suffering and endurance, the conviction of being in support of a great act of God, and he saw the hardship, the deprivation, and the honor. Notice the soldiers, their dress and weaponry, and the determination their faces portray. Those qualities are the external expression of the conviction of conscience that brought thirteen diverse and distant colonies together to form a nation.

Could that happen again today? What are the essentials of the idea of self-government? The themes in *Nation Makers* Part II give the "big picture."

You may have been taught God's Principle of Individuality

Nation Makers by Howard Pyle

as early as kindergarten and every year of your education so far. If so, good for you, because it is the basic principle of all principles by which to live. You may also have studied the Chain of Christianity® throughout your schooling. If so, you have a general framework for learning everything else you will ever learn.

However, *Nation Makers* is your opportunity to go deeper in understanding and embracing these essential concepts as you prepare for higher levels of study.

What do you already know about God's Principle of Individuality and the Chain of Christianity?

God's Principle of Individuality

From our study of the record of Creation, we learn that God filled the "void" with a Creation that had shape, form, and identity. It seems significant that God distinguished each aspect of Creation and named and identified everything that He created—and He created everything.

Contrast this with the theory of evolution where all things are supposed to start from non-life and painfully work up to the immense variety of incredibly complex plant, human, and animal life forms.

God created and completed the identity—the distinct "kind" of all things—and He both classified and individualized everything that He made. God never makes two things alike—He never repeats himself. Because He is the Infinite One—His Infinity, Diversity, and Individuality are expressed throughout His Creation. Yet, despite the infinite vastness and immensity of God, not one thing that He creates is out of His sight.

> "ARE NOT TWO SPARROWS SOLD FOR A PENNY? AND NOT ONE OF THEM SHALL FALL ON THE GROUND APART FROM YOUR FATHER. BUT EVEN THE HAIRS OF YOUR HEAD ARE ALL NUMBERED."
> MATTHEW 10:29, 30 (ESV)

God's Principle of Individuality makes each one of us distinct and unique. We see this from the obvious evidence of no two faces alike—ever—and the pattern of our fingerprints. Dr. Roger J. Williams, Professor of Biochemistry at the University of Texas, made a lifelong study of individuality. He has accumulated much data to document that each one of us is individual in every detail of our bodies—from the size and shape of every organ, the length, placement and arrangement of our nervous system, to our sleeping, eating, and exercising patterns. In fact, the more one studies God's universe, the more one becomes convinced that God has put His stamp of individuality upon everything that He created.

God's Principle of Individuality is a key to the study of history and this key delivers a staggering blow to evolution. This principle can be seen in evidence if one accepts the Biblical basis of Creation and acknowledges that God shaped all things for His own purpose. Thus continents, nations, and men have a part in God's plan for history—His Story.

A close look at nature in God's universe discovers the many unique and wonderful things that He has created for His pleasure and divine purpose. Nothing gives more joy than the knowledge that the Creator specially designs each one of us for eternity, possessing an individual purpose, unique to our personhood in Christ. However, without Christ, the special gift of individuality is easily abused and wasted and becomes self-centered individualism. It is essential to understand that the Gospel alone can govern our individuality and channel it towards our created purpose.

When we learn to govern individually by character and conscience and to relate to others with those principles, we are properly self-governed and our individuality fully cultivated.

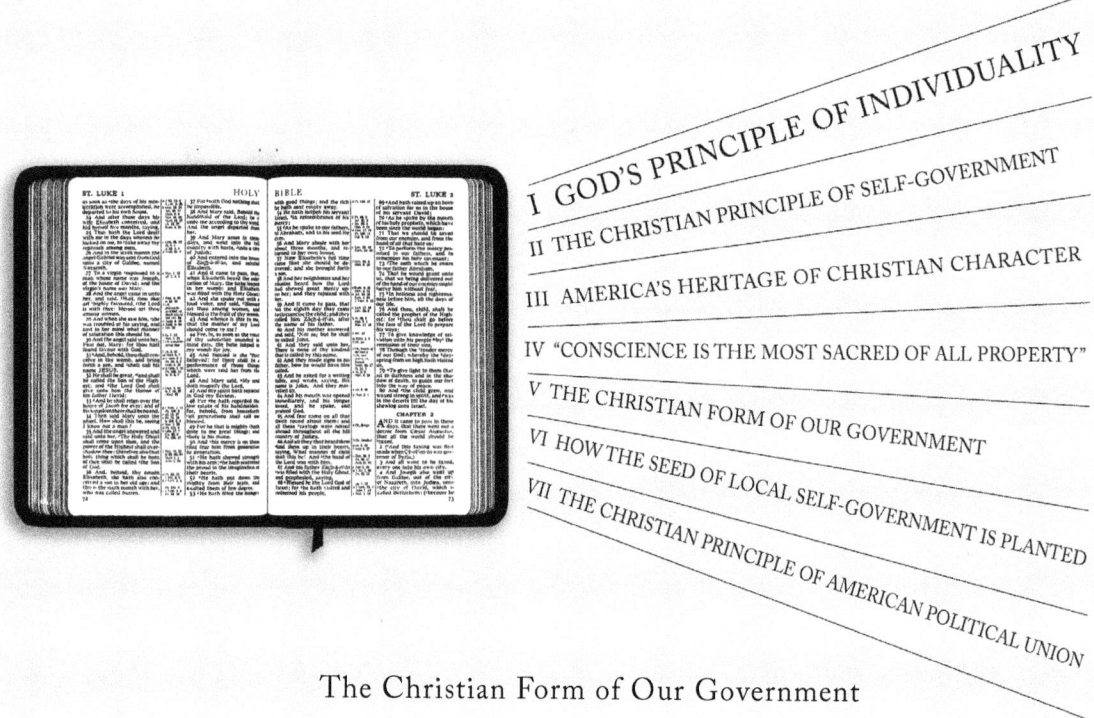

The Christian Form of Our Government

Geographic Individuals: Not only are we specifically designed individually for God's purposes, God's purpose can be seen in the design of the continents of the earth. Arnold Guyot,[1] a Christian geographer, makes the following statement as he looks at God's earth:

"It belongs not to man to read in the future the decrees of Providence. But science may attempt to comprehend the purpose of God, as to the destinies *of* nations, by examining with care the theatre, seemingly arranged by Him...."

How does Mr. Guyot explain the arrangement of the geographic features of the earth?

What does God's Principle of Individuality mean to you personally?

Geographic Individuality

"ASIA is the largest of the continents, the most central, the only one with which all the others are closely connected; and the one whose different physical regions show the strongest contrasts, and are separated by the greatest barriers....

"... This great and strongly marked continent is the *continent of origins*. The human family, its races and civilizations, and the systems of religion that rule the most enlightened nations, all had their beginning here.

"By the great *diversity of its physical features* and climate, and the strong barriers isolating them one from another, Asia was admirably fitted to promote the formation of a diversity of races; while its close connection with the other continents facilitated their dispersion throughout the earth...."

---

1 R.J. Slater, *Teaching and Learning America's Christian History: The Principle Approach* (FACE, 2005), 142-153.

Baptism of Pocahontas by John Gadsby Chapman

How did the geographic factors of the continent of Asia help bring about the diversity of the races?

"EUROPE shows a *diversity of structure* even greater than that of Asia; but with smaller areas, more moderate forms of relief, less extreme contrasts of climate, a more generally fertile soil, and everywhere an abundance of the most useful minerals; while the relative extent of its coast line, its maritime zone is greater than that of any other continent.

"This continent is especially fitted, by its diversity, to foster the formation of distinct nationalities, each developing in an especial direction. Moreover, the proximity of these nations one to another, the greater facility of communication between them, and, above all, the common highway to the sea, nowhere very distant, facilitates mutual intercourse, the lack of which arrested the progress of the civilization of Asia....

"… Though not the continent of origins, Europe is emphatically the *continent of development.* The Indo-European *race* the people of progress find their fullest expansion and activity, not in their original seat in Iran, but in Europe, whence they are spreading over all the quarters of the globe. The *arts* and *learning* of antiquity attained their highest development, not in western Asia and Egypt, the places of their origin, but in Greece and Rome.

"*Christianity*, also, only germinated in western Asia. Transplanted to Europe, it gradually attained its full development, and became the foundation on which is reared the vast and noble edifice of modern civilization."

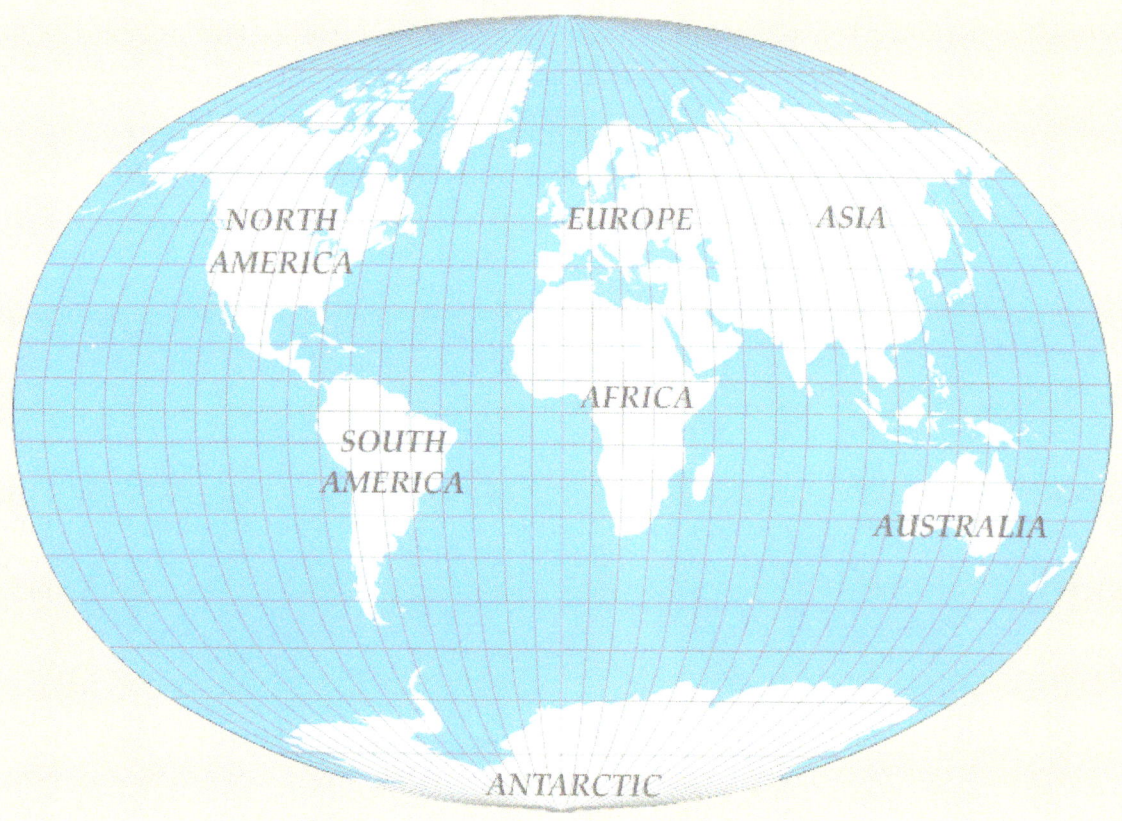

✎ What developed as Christianity moved westward into Europe?

How did the geographic factors of the continent of Europe help bring about the development of nationalities?

"AMERICA, different in position, structure, and climatic conditions, from both the other northern continents, seems destined to play a part in the history of mankind unlike that of Europe and Asia, though not less noble than either.

"The *structure* of this continent … is characterized by a unity and simplicity as striking as is the diversity of Europe.…

"In its *climate*, those contrasts in temperature which are so violent in Asia, and still prevail in Europe, are obliterated.… .

"… Nowhere do we find in America those local centers, each having a strongly marked individuality, which fostered the progress of the race in its infancy and its youth; but everywhere provision is made for mutual intercourse, a common life, and the blending of the entire population into one. Evidently this continent was not designed to give birth and development to a new civilization; but to receive one ready-made, and to furnish to the cultivated race of the Old World the scene most worthy of their activity.

"Its vast plains, overflowing with natural wealth, are turned towards Europe, and its largest rivers discharge into the Atlantic; while its lofty mountains, and less fertile lands, are removed far towards its western shores. Thus it seems to invite the Indo-European race, the people of progress, to new fields of action; to encourage their expansion throughout its entire territory, and their fusion into one nation; while it opens for them a pathway to all the nations of the earth.

"America, therefore, with her cultured and progressive people, and her social organization, founded upon the principle of the equality and brotherhood of all mankind, seems destined to furnish *the most complete expression of the Christian civilization*; and to become the fountain of a new and higher life for all the races of men."

Why did Christianity have to move westward to the American continent?

What geographic features in the North American continent helped it become the continent where Christianity can offer a higher life for all the races and nationalities of mankind?

"Conclusion. Each continent has, therefore, a well-defined individuality, which fits it for an especial function. The fullness of nature's life is typified by Africa, with its superabundant wealth and power of animal life; South America, with its exuberance of vegetation; and Australia, with its antiquated forms of plants and animals.

"In the grand drama of *man's life* and development, Asia, Europe, and America play distinct parts, for which each seems to have been admirably prepared.

"Truly no blind force gave our Earth the forms so well adapted to perform these functions."

The emphatic conclusion is irresistible that the entire globe is a grand organism, every feature of which is the outgrowth of a definite plan of the all-wise Creator for the education of the human family, and the manifestation of his own glory. [Arnold Guyot, *Physical Geography*]

Write the emphatic conclusion to Geographic Individuality in your notes.

Providential History

PROVIDENCE, n. foresight; timely care; the care and superintendence which God exercises over his creatures.

PROVIDEN´TIAL, a. Effected by the providence of God; proceeding from divine direction or superintendence. How much are we indebted to God's unceasing providential care!

HIS´TORY, n. 1. An account of facts, particularly of facts respecting nations or states; a narration of events in the order in which they happened, with their causes and effects.

Discuss the definitions above and the memory tree of Providential History below.

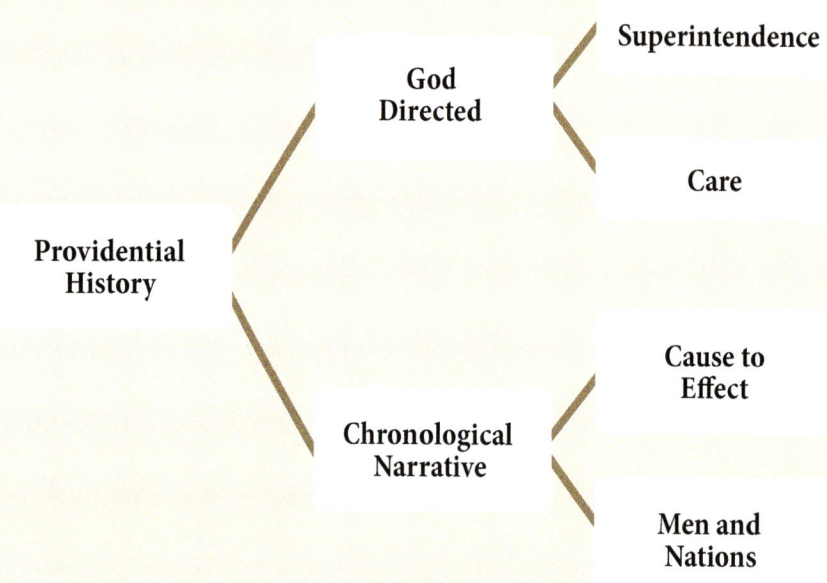

 Copy the providential history memory tree in your notebook to help you remember the definition.

Seeing history through the lens of God's Hand directing men and nations for His purposes could be termed "His Story." Great wisdom comes from this view of history to instruct us today. When we study history, we are informing ourselves of what came before, establishing a "memory" of experiences that can be learned to guide our discernment of right and wrong, of consequences, and of how to think from an eternal perspective about what is happening today.

Other Definitions of History

Knowing history imparts wisdom to us today as we learn the lessons of the past in the context of their causes and effects – acts and consequences. Discuss the definitions of history that follow, from famous authors of literature and history.

Which ones best define history for you? Which one best defines providential history?

1. "History is the essence of innumerable Biographies."—*Carlyle*
2. "History is philosophy learned from examples."—*Dionysius of Halicarnassus*
3. "History, by apprising (men) of the past, will enable them to judge of the future."—*Thomas Jefferson*
4. "We may gather out of history a policy no less wise than eternal; by the comparison and application of other men's forepassed miseries with our own like errors and ill deservings." —*Sir Walter Raleigh*
5. "History, with all her volumes vast, Hath but *one* page."—*Byron*
6. "The use of history is to give value to the present hour and its duty."—*Emerson*
7. "To be ignorant of what happened before you were born is to be ever a child. For what is man's lifetime unless the memory of past events is woven with those of earlier times?"—*Cicero*

8. "The principal office of history I take to be this: to prevent virtuous actions from being forgotten, and that evil words and deeds should fear an infamous reputation with posterity."—*Tacitus*

9. "Ancient histories, as one of our wits has said, are but fables that have been agreed upon."—*Voltaire*

10. "History is, indeed, little more than the register of the crimes, follies, and misfortunes of mankind." —*Gibbon*

11. "The history of all hitherto existing society is the history of class struggles."—*Karl Marx*

12. "It is the true office of history to represent the events themselves, together with the counsels, and to leave the observations and conclusions thereupon to the liberty and faculty of every man's judgment." —*Bacon*

13. "To be a really good historian is perhaps the rarest of intellectual disciplines."—*Macaulay*

14. "It has been said that history is the biography of communities; in another, and profounder, sense, it is the autobiography of him 'Who worketh all things after the counsel of his own will' (Ephesians 1:11), and who is graciously timing all events in the interests of his Christ, and of the kingdom of God on earth." —*Rev. S. W. Foljambe*

15. "History is a form of wisdom." — *Mr. Ben Gilmore*

Write your own understanding of providential history.

Understanding God's Hand in Human History
Chart created from content in "Nation Making" by John Fiske 1889 (*CHOC* page 10)

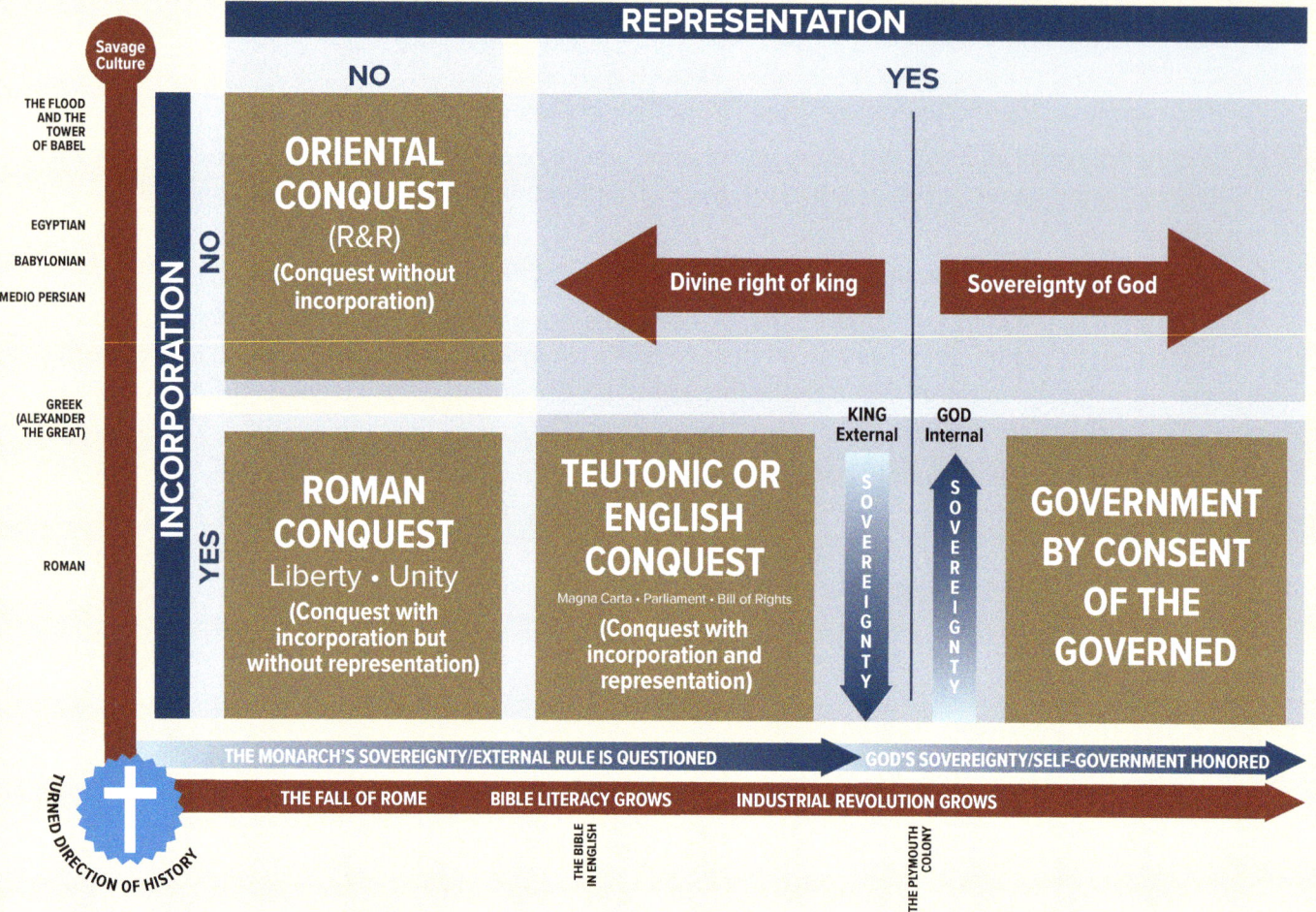

Mr. Ben Gilmore of Sacramento, California has developed the above fascinating chart called "Understanding God's Hand in Human History" that he explains in the following article:

God's Hand in Human History
By Mr. Ben Gilmore, Christian History Study Groups

It all began with an article on "Nation Making" in John Fiske's "The Beginnings of New England" 1889. (*CHOC* page 10) I drew a two by two chart in my notes. The chart demonstrated the four possible combinations of "Incorporation" and "Representation." As I contemplated what Mr. Fiske had taught me, this paper grew out of it. Everything we will ever learn about events and periods in human history can be found on this chart in the context of what God is teaching mankind.

In the beginning of civilization a guy and a girl get together and make a family. That family becomes the "building block" of every civilization. Several families get together to share the tasks of life, gathering food, cooking, protection, etc. Let us call it "savage culture."

Every family has a concept of a "higher power." Let us call the vertical relationship between families and that higher power, "church." Further – every culture has a relationship between families and families. Let us call that horizontal relationship, "civil-government" or "state." This is universal for all cultures, pagan or Christian, historic or modern. These three human organizations are the only human organizations I have found in the Bible that God ordained and through which He deals with man.

In civilizations, the dominant concept of the vertical relationship with God or "god" will always determine the horizontal quality of state. Note- Throughout history it is never the other way around. The state never successfully establishes the vertical relationship. It is a law of nature.

The Creator God of the Bible wants to teach mankind to love Him (vertical), then to love one another (horizontal). Man is a slow learner! It took Christ 1620 years to make a Pilgrim! It has taken humans centuries of trial and error to grow from age to age.

Fiske describes the earliest growth from savage culture to "Oriental Conquest." Oriental Conquest is defined as having no incorporation and no representation. I describe it as rape and ravage. Think of Genghis Kahn, a tribal leader with the biggest club. One day he is looking across the river at a neighbor's territory. He gets his guys together and builds a raft. They cross the river and plunder what they want, clubbing anyone who objects. Halfway home he turns and shouts, "We'll be back in six months. Have another stack of plunder ready for us."

Genghis Kahn takes no part in how they raise the tribute (i.e. they are not incorporated into his government). Neither are they represented in his government. That is "Oriental Conquest" – No Incorporation and no Representation.

The last example of oriental conquest is with Alexander the Great during the 400 year gap in Bible history between the Old and New Testament. He was a Greek conqueror. Greek philosophers said you could not form a large government under one umbrella. Even the Greek city-states could not get along with one another!

God did an interesting thing in those days. Alexander was a great military tactician. He overhauled the Greek language into a military language called "koine Greek," so that his orders would be clearly understood. Alexander went on to conquer the then known world. I am told that the koine Greek dialect is the most succinct of all human languages. God used that language to write the New Testament.

Along came the Romans. They said, "Yes, you can sustain an umbrella government! When a Roman staff is planted in your city square, you just moved within Rome city limits!" Roman law, Roman culture, Roman roads, Roman language – everything became "Roman."

Fiske calls it "Roman Conquest," Incorporation without Representation. This was a giant step above "Oriental Conquest." At the beginning, Roman government functioned well, until internal corruption and lack of allegiance among the conquered nations caused degradation. This is illustrated in the Jewish relations with Rome in the New Testament.

The Romans spread out even further than had Alexander. Their concept of government involved a top-down form of unity and liberty that had not been seen before. They covered Alexander's world plus Europe and most of what were later the British Isles – except for Scotland. Scotts today will proudly point to what remains of a wall the Romans never crossed.

While all this was going on in the Middle East and Mediterranean area, a branch of civilization had moved northward and established a culture of its own in Scandinavia (Norway, Sweden, Finland, and Denmark). They were called the Teutonic races. Think of Leif Erikson, horned fur hats, and longboat explorers.

The Teutonic tribes had an interesting culture. They held council meetings around a flat rock on a hilltop. When they conquered another tribe, the leaders of the conquered tribe were included in the council meeting. Suppose your tribe had just been conquered. You could see the hilltop fire at the council meeting and your leader was there! You, little you, were represented!

In Oriental or even Roman Conquest, your only value was in your worth to your ruler. In the Teutonic culture you had intrinsic value – you had a representative! Imagine how that was received when a Christian evangelist

told them Christ would represent them before God. Christianity was spreading throughout the world.

Back to Roman Conquest – The Roman city limit was spread broader and broader. The Roman Army that was spread thinner and thinner defended it. Things inside the Roman border were better than things outside. There were growing attacks from outside, while corruption within was also growing. In the midst of the Roman Conquest era, was the advent of Christ. That one life would change forever the direction of civilization.

Governments, like individuals, have a built in policy of self-defense. As pressure on Roman government grew, "liberty" was sacrificed to keep "unity." They began recalling the army to protect a shrinking border.

The natives of the soon to be "British Isles" invited the Teutonic tribes to come help drive out the Romans (who were leaving anyway!). The Teutons were happy to oblige. They went on to take over the Islands. They became the Saxons. They brought their Teutonic culture with them.

Rome fell and civilization drifted backwards into the Middle-ages. Some call it the "Dark-ages," but they weren't dark at all. God was at work. Monks in monasteries were making copies of the Bible and preserving it. Christianity continued spreading.

A King named Charlemagne began trying to rebuild the Holy Roman Empire. He was disappointed when some Teutonic tribes sailed down into what was to become the English Channel and landed on the Normandy coast. Unlike their cousins the Saxons, they adopted the Roman or Latin culture. Think of Leif Erikson with velvet vest and lace on his sleeves.

As time passed, the Normans attacked their relatives, the Saxons, and some of them moved to Britain to coexist. If you have read of "Ivanhoe" or "Robin Hood" – they were Saxons. The sheriff was a Norman. They had to find a way to get along. The Roman top down culture grinding against the Saxon idea of individual worth. Out of that grinding, with seeds of Christianity mixed in, came the Magna Charta, then the Parliament and the English Bill of Rights. Incorporation with Representation. Fiske calls it "Teutonic or English Conquest."

Common men were reading the Bible. Literacy exploded on the scene. Men were reasoning from the Bible. The question arose, "Who or what is in charge?" Is the King law, or is the Law king? The concept of sovereignty was shifting from man to God. That concept bridged the Atlantic Ocean to America where God and "We the people" created government by consent of the governed.

Please ponder the associated chart, "Understanding God's Hand in Human History." Note that it is based upon Fiske's 2x2 matrix – Incorporation & Representation. Note the major changes that developed when Incorporation with Representation was included in government. Now consider that the advent of Jesus Christ was the root cause of all of that!

Write your understanding of the chart (see p. 48) in a summary in your notebook.

Nation Making: Methods and Results[2]

Read each paragraph, identifying the key thought of each and writing the key thought in a sentence.

1. "As in all the achievements of mankind, it is only after much weary experiment and many a heart-sickening failure that success is attained, so has it been especially with nation-making. Skill in the political art is the fruit of ages of intellectual and moral discipline; and just as picture-writing had to come before printing and canoes before steamboats, so the **cruder political methods had to be tried and found wanting**, amid the tears and groans of unnumbered generations, before methods less crude could be put into operation....

---

[2] V.M. Hall, *The Christian History of the Constitution of the United States of America: Christian Self-Government*, Vol. I (FACE, 2006), 10-16.

2. "In welding together of primitive shifting tribes into stable and powerful nations, we can seem to discern three different methods that have been followed at different times and places, with widely different results. In all cases the fusion has been effected by war, but it has gone on in three broadly contrasting ways. **The first** of these methods, which has been followed from time immemorial in the Oriental world, may be roughly described as *conquest without incorporation*. A tribe grows to national dimensions by conquering and annexing its neighbors, without admitting them to a share in its political life. Probably there is always at first some incorporation, or even perhaps some crude germ of federative alliance; but this goes very little way, only far enough to fuse together a few closely related tribes, agreeing in speech and habits, into a single great tribe that can overwhelm its neighbors. In early society this sort of incorporation cannot go far without being stopped by some impassable barrier of language or religion. After reaching this point, the conquering tribe simply annexes its neighbors and makes them its slaves. It becomes a superior caste, ruling over vanquished peoples, whom it oppresses with frightful cruelty, while living on the fruits of their toil in what has been aptly termed Oriental luxury.… In this first method of nation-making, then, which we may call the **Oriental method**, one now sees but little to commend.

3. "The **second method** by which nations have been made may be called the Roman method; and we may briefly describe it as *conquest with incorporation, but without representation*. The secret of Rome's wonderful strength lay in the fact that she incorporated the vanquished peoples into her own body politic.… Never before had so many people been brought under one government without making slaves of most of them. Liberty had existed before, whether in barbaric tribes or in Greek cities. Union had existed before, in Assyrian or Persian despotisms. Now liberty and union were for the first time joined together, with consequences enduring and stupendous. The whole Mediterranean world was brought under one government; ancient barriers of religion, speech, and custom were overthrown in every direction; and innumerable barbarian tribes, from the Alps to the wilds of northern Britain, from the Bay of Biscay to the Carpathian Mountains, were more or less completely transformed into Roman citizens, protected by Roman law, and sharing in the material and spiritual benefits of Roman civilization.

4. "The Roman method of nation-making lacked the principle of representation. The old Roman world knew nothing of representative assemblies. Its senates were assemblies of notables, constituting in the main an aristocracy of men who had held high office; its popular assemblies were primary assemblies, town meetings. There was no notion of such a thing as political power delegated by the people to representatives who were to wield it away from home and out of sight of their constituents. The Roman's only notion of delegated power was that of authority delegated by the government to its generals and prefects who discharged at a distance its military and civil functions. When, therefore, the Roman popular government, originally adapted to a single city, had come to extend itself over a large part of the world, it lacked the one institution by means of which government could be carried on over so vast an area without degenerating into despotism.…

5. "The third method of nation-making may be called the Teutonic or preeminently the English method. It differs from the Oriental and Roman methods which we have been considering in a feature of most profound significance; it **contains the principle of representation**. For this reason, though like all nation-making it was in its early stages attended with war and conquest, it nevertheless does not necessarily require war and conquest in order to be put into operation. Of the other two methods war was an essential part.… We have seen, nevertheless, that for want of representation the Roman method failed when applied to an immense territory, and the government tended to become more and more despotic, to revert toward the Oriental type.

6. "Our experience has now so far widened that we can see that **despotism is not the strongest but well nigh the weakest form of government**; that centralized administrations, like that of the Roman Empire, have fallen to pieces, not because of too much but because of too little freedom; and that the only perdurable government must be that which succeeds in achieving national unity on a grand scale, without weakening

the sense of personal and local independence. For in the body politic this spirit of freedom is as the red corpuscles in the blood; it carries the life with it. It makes the difference between a society of self-respecting men and women and a society of puppets. Your nation may have art, poetry, and science, all the refinements of civilized life, all the comforts and safeguards that human ingenuity can devise; but if it lose this spirit of personal and local independence, it is doomed and deserves its doom....

7. "The <u>fundamental principle of political freedom</u> is 'no taxation without representation'; you must not take a farthing of my money without consulting my wishes as to the use that shall be made of it. Only when this principle of justice was first practically recognized, did government begin to divorce itself from the primitive bestial barbaric system of tyranny and plunder, and to ally itself with the forces that in the fulness of time are to bring peace on earth and good will to men. Of all dates in history, therefore, there is none more fit to be commemorated than 1265; for in that year there was first asserted and applied at Westminster, on a national scale, that fundamental principle of 'no taxation without representation', that <u>innermost kernel of the English Idea</u>, which the Stamp Act Congress defended at New York exactly five hundred years afterward. . . . . **The inherited predatory tendency of men** to seize upon the fruits of other people's labor is still very strong, and while we have nothing more to fear from kings, we may yet have trouble enough from commercial monopolies and favoured industries, marching to the polls their hordes of bribed retainers. **Well indeed has it been said that eternal vigilance is the price of liberty.** God never meant that in this fair but treacherous world in which He placed us we should earn our salvation without steadfast labour. [John Fiske, *The Beginnings of New England or the Puritan Theocracy in its Relations to Civil and Religious Liberty*, Boston, MA: Houghton, Mifflin and Company, 1898, 4–13, 16–21, 24–27]."

What is the result of the oriental method? While Rome did not make slaves of all the nations she conquered, what did her method of government lack?

This explanation of the types of nation-making demonstrated in history is seen by a providential perspective. Secular history is essentially a list of facts interpreted by the human perspective of the moment without recognizing the hand of God. Learning to identify the difference between secular history and providential history is an important discernment to cultivate. As we begin to look more deeply into the blessings of self-government, we will begin by examining a model of providential history from a nineteenth century textbook. It is important to note that prior to the twentieth century, most history was written as providential history! Let's look closely at an account of Creation from a providential perspective:

A Model of Providential History[3]

For many decades Mrs. Emma Willard's history textbook was the standard of the study of history by American students. It is a model of providential history.

Preface

"Universal history, as a science, is great in its consequences, as it forms the first study of the politician. No wise man presumes to form conclusions concerning the future destiny of nations, without first acquiring a knowledge of the past. It is at this time peculiarly important to Americans; because to them nations of the world are now looking for a response to the grand question, 'Can the people govern themselves?' And, perhaps, the next twenty years will decide it for coming generations. Shall monarchy in its palaces, and aristocracy in its lordly halls, then exult, as it is told that America is passing through anarchy to despotism— while mankind at large mourn, and reproach us that we have sealed their doom as well as our own, and that of our posterity? Or shall we continue to be that people, which of all others heretofore, or now existing, possess the most equitable government; and to whom national calamity is but as a phrase ill understood? A history of the past, no more extensive than that which is here presented, might make us understand that

---

3 Emma Willard, *Universal History in Perspective: Divided into Three Parts, Ancient, Middle, and Modern* A.S. Barnes & Co., New York, 1855).

phrase, with a salutary fear; and it might teach our posterity what we as good citizens must desire them to know—the virtues which exalt nations, and the vices which destroy them;—so they may practice the one, and avoid the other."

Notice the wisdom this history presents. Identify two wise maxims in the above selection.

Chapter I

From the Creation, 4004 B.C.—To the Tower of Babel, 2300 B.C.

"1. The face of the whole earth, with a few exceptions, is now known. The family of man is divided by natural distinctions, into different races; and by the boundary lines of the countries that they inhabit, into different nations, each governed by its own peculiar laws.

"2. If we take a map representing the entire world, and inquire concerning the length of time, which the nations it now presents have been known, we shall find in looking back to different periods, that by degrees, their names and places disappear. In A.D. 1491, the whole continent of America was, as to those from whom we derive the knowledge of history, as though it were not. A little before the birth of our Savior, Great Britain, the land of our ancestors, was unknown, as was the whole of the northern part of Europe, the southern part of Africa, and the eastern part of Asia. If we go back 2000 years from the Christian era, no traces of inhabitants are to be found on the face of the earth, except a few comparatively small nations, near the eastern extremity of the Mediterranean Sea.

"3. Hence, even without referring to the sacred writings, we should conclude, that the human race probably had their origin in that region; and calculating their progress from what is known of later times, we should also conclude that they might have been, supposing they commenced with a single family, about two thousand years from the period last mentioned in coming to the state in which we then find them. But it is upon the sacred writings alone, that we depend for historical information concerning the creation, and first abode of the human race. These, the calculations of Scripture dates most approved by the learned, fix at 4004 years before the Christian era, and in the region east of the Mediterranean Sea. Thus we find our confidence in the truth of the Sacred Scriptures, greatly strengthened by a comprehensive view of universal history."

Read Genesis 1 and 2. Then discuss Mrs. Willard's following description of beginnings, in light of the Bible's account.

"4. Those nations which have not possessed the Scriptures have held traditions concerning gods and goddesses, and the origin of men and things, full of monstrous absurdities. Some men, calling themselves philosophers, have, in the pride of their own fancied wisdom, rejected the Scriptures, and have undertaken to make out systems of the world from conjecture; and, by their ridiculous theories, they have made themselves the jest of succeeding ages. Supposing changes more miraculous than any related in Scripture, they have not assigned any power, adequate to their production.

"5. In the infancy of the human species, God appears to have dealt with man, in a manner, different from the ordinary course of his providence, at the present day. An earthly parent is more with his helpless and ignorant children, than with those who have experience. The first duty which he teaches them, is implicit obedience to his will; and when he finds them wayward and disobedient, he chastises them, and sometimes, with severity. Thus, as the Scriptures inform us, did the Almighty Parent deal with man, in the infant state of his being."

Part II: The Blessing of Self-Government

Identify Mrs. Willard's providential view in paragraphs 4 and 5.

The Transgression, Punishment, and Promise

"6. Adam and Eve, whom God had created in his own image, pure and holy, disobeyed his command, and were driven from their first abode, the beautiful garden of Eden. On the day of their disobedience, the sentence of death was passed upon them. The man was condemned to earn his bread by the sweat of his brow; and the woman, who had been seduced by flattery and undue curiosity, to be the first transgressor, was punished with a double curse. Yet did God, in his mercy, then promise, that of her seed should ONE arise, to bruise the head of the deceiver. Thus, according to MOSES, the promise of a SAVIOR was coeval with the fall of man, and his need of a Redeemer.

"7. We are informed that the life of man, before the deluge, extended to ten times its present period. Most of the knowledge, now possessed by the human race, is derived from the experience and observation of the men who have lived before them; but in those days there were no such stores of knowledge laid up. A life of several hundred years would give each man time to learn much from his own experience, and thus facilitate the general improvement of the race. Hence it seems very natural to suppose, that God should have allotted to men a longer period of existence at the first. As there are no authorities to consult on this part of history, except the sacred volume, which is, or should be in the hands of every one, we shall refer the student to that for particular facts; mentioning only those which are more immediately connected with the course of events, as detailed by those historians, who, in distinction from the *sacred*, are termed *profane* writers."

The Dove Sent Forth from the Ark

What can we learn from a view of providential history that is not learned from looking at history without the benefit of seeing God's hand? Is a secular view of history helpful to impart wisdom for life?

Individual Links on the Chain of His Story

Nation Makers: the Art of Self-Government deals with two major themes that represent the principles undergirding the establishment of America as a nation governed by a Christian Constitution. The first theme we study as we move westward with the spread of Christianity is the consideration of "**How are men governed?**"

Since the occurrence of man's first disobedience and his fall, there has been a constant effort by mankind to establish a government to hold in check the wickedness of man and man's inhumanity to man. At the same time as Christianity was related to the civil sphere, the concept of individual liberty became more widespread and thus, increased the desire to restrain the power of government over those it governed. This resulted in a constant teeter tottering of the power of government—sometimes it resided in a king or emperor, sometimes it was taken into the hands of the people.

It took 1620 years from the time our Lord appeared for Christian liberty to be seen fully as God-given, not government-granted. The Pilgrims understood that government is first <u>internal,</u> as each individual accepts the liberty that only Jesus Christ can give. It is <u>external</u> in the civil sphere. Christian self-government requires less restriction from external government and allows greater freedom in the life of the individual.

As we study the unfolding of this concept of government along the Chain of Christianity®, we shall see some glimmerings of freedom for the individual. But it was only as Christianity reached the North American continent that this aspect of Christian self-government was most fully expressed in the civil sphere. As the Pilgrims considered themselves as "stepping stones" for "[the] propagating & advancing [the] Gospel of [the] kingdom of Christ in those remote parts of [the] world," so they also became the founding fathers of the Christian principles of government that later were incorporated into our American Constitution.

A second major theme that we shall consider along the Chain of Christianity is **individual character** and how it is used by God to forward His Story. After Christ our Lord appears, it becomes more than conscientious obedience to God's laws and character becomes related to individual salvation and the putting off of "the old man, which is corrupt," and the putting on of the "new man, which after God is created in righteousness and true holiness."

What is the significance of the George Herbert quote below?

RELIGION STANDS ON TIP-TOE IN OUR LAND

READY TO PASS TO THE AMERICAN STRAND.

GEORGE HERBERT

TIME LINES: Leaders; Bible in English; Events
*How the Reformers, with the translation of the Bible into English,
led to the establishment of a self-governing nation in America*

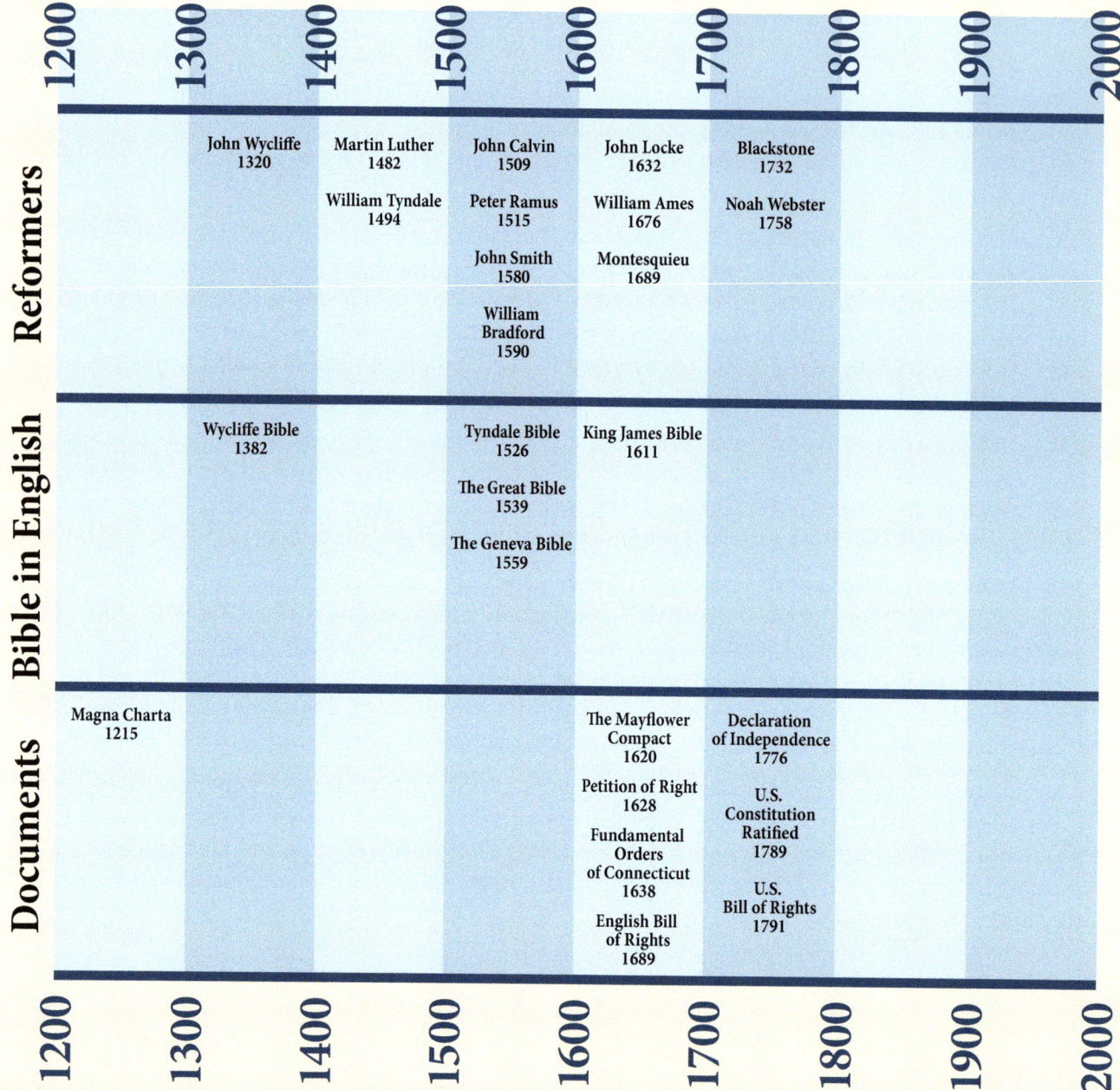

	1200	1300	1400	1500	1600	1700	1800	1900	2000
Reformers		John Wycliffe 1320	Martin Luther 1482; William Tyndale 1494	John Calvin 1509; Peter Ramus 1515; John Smith 1580; William Bradford 1590	John Locke 1632; William Ames 1676; Montesquieu 1689	Blackstone 1732; Noah Webster 1758			
Bible in English		Wycliffe Bible 1382		Tyndale Bible 1526; The Great Bible 1539; The Geneva Bible 1559	King James Bible 1611				
Documents	Magna Charta 1215				The Mayflower Compact 1620; Petition of Right 1628; Fundamental Orders of Connecticut 1638; English Bill of Rights 1689	Declaration of Independence 1776; U.S. Constitution Ratified 1789; U.S. Bill of Rights 1791			

Chain of Christianity® Moves Westward

This list of names, events, and nations is not intended to be exhaustive, but rather indicative of the fact that God used men and nations through Christ to bring forth America and her form of government, for His glory and for all the nations of the earth.

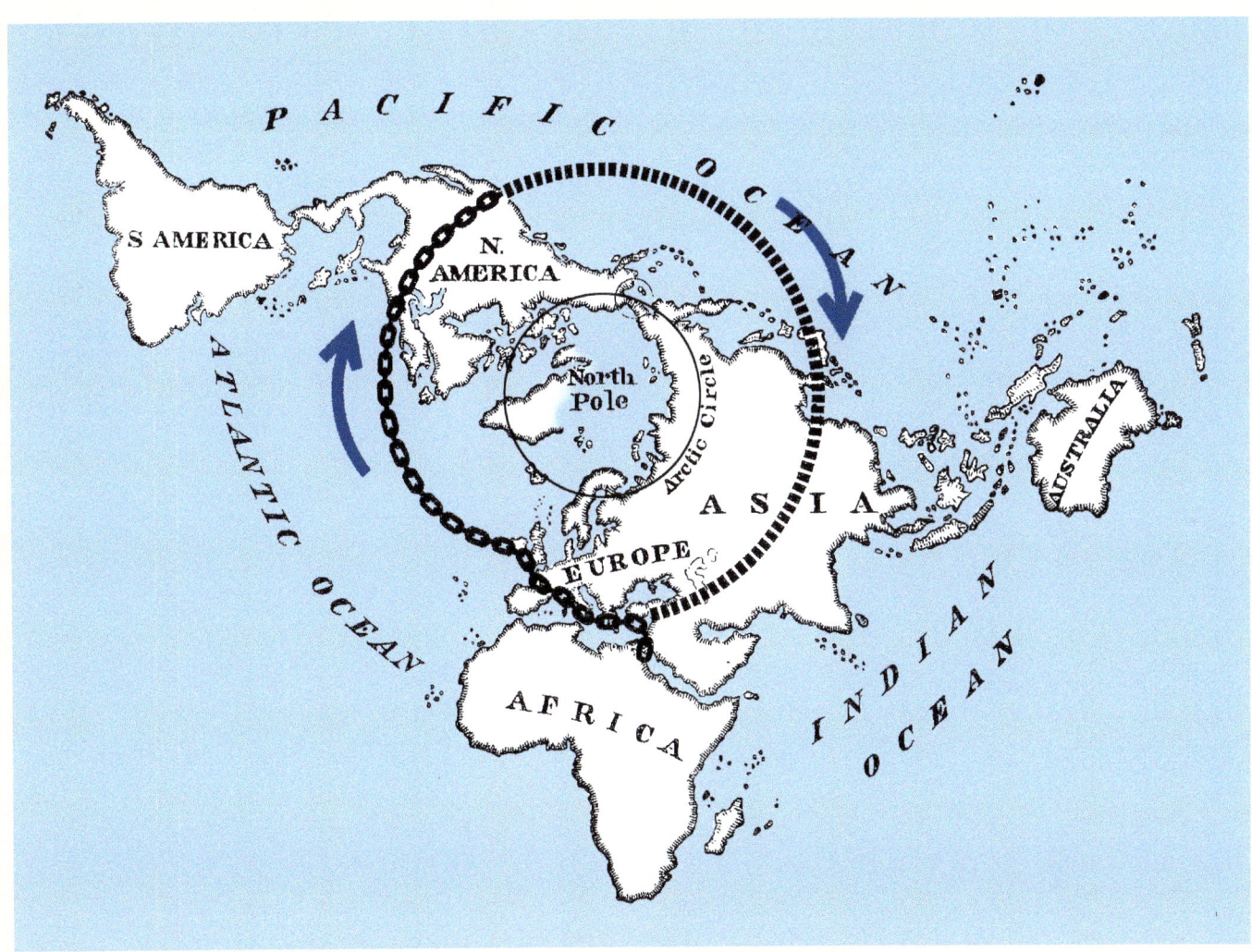

Creation
Natural & Revealed Law
Jesus Christ & Gospel

First Century
Apostles & Disciples
Paul's Missionary Journeys

First Westward Planting of Seeds of Christianity
Rome
Greece
Europe

Second Century
France
Spain
Britain
Germany

Fourth Century
Jerome 340
Augustine 354
Ireland— Patrick 389
Alfred 848-901

Morning Stars of Reformation
Magna Charta 1215
Wycliffe 1324
Jan Hus 1369
Johann Gutenberg 1396
Martin Luther 1483
Ulrich Zwingli 1484
Hugh Latimer 1485
Miles Coverdale 1488
William Tyndale 1494
John Knox 1505
John Calvin 1509
Peter Ramus 1515
John Fox 1516
Gaspard De Coligny 1519
Richard Hooker 1554

Prelude to America
Geneva Bible 1557
William Brewster 1563
John Robinson 1575
William Ames 1576
Hugo Grotius 1583
Thomas Hooker 1586
John Winthrop 1588
William Bradford 1590
Richard Mather 1596
John Milton 1608

America's Planting
Jamestown 1607
King James Bible 1611
Mayflower Compact 1620
Pilgrims Land at Plymouth 1620
Petition of Right 1628
John Bunyan 1628
William Penn 1644
English Bill of Rights 1689
Locke's Treatise on Government 1689

Christopher Dock 1698
Jonathan Edwards 1703
John & Charles Wesley 1703, 1707
George Whitefield 1714
Montesquieu The Spirit of Laws 1748
Blackstone's Commentaries 1765

Foundation of a New Nation
The Declaration of Independence 1776
The Constitution of the United States of America 1787
The Monroe Doctrine 1823

Part II Essay: "The Hand of God in Human History"

ESSAY Explain the Hand-of-God-in-Human-History chart on page 48 in your own words using cause-to-effect reasoning. What does this mean to you in terms of the blessing of self-government?

Nation Makers
Part III:
The Nature of Law

| Natural and Revealed Law | Moral Law | Civil Law | Democracy | Republic | Two Systems |

Natural and Revealed Law

God established law at Creation to govern His universe. God's laws governed the physical world from the moment of Creation; they hold the world together. To our eyes the sun "rises" every morning. However, closer observation proves that the sun does not "rise"; in actuality, Earth revolves around the sun making it appear to rise. By observation and reason, man can identify the many physical laws God set in place at Creation. You can name many of these "natural laws" that have been identified over millennia by observation and reason. Natural laws also govern the spirit of man and are inherent in every individual.

Everything in the universe and in heaven is governed by a specific set of laws that the Creator put in place at Creation. We learn in life that if we stay within God's law, we experience the blessings of life, peace and growth. If we step outside God's laws, we experience chaos. Let's begin this part of *Nation Makers* by defining LAW:

 LAW, n. In general, law is a rule of action prescribed for the government of rational beings or moral agents, to which rule they are bound to yield obedience, in default of which they are exposed to punishment; or law is a settled mode or course of action or operation in irrational beings and in inanimate bodies.

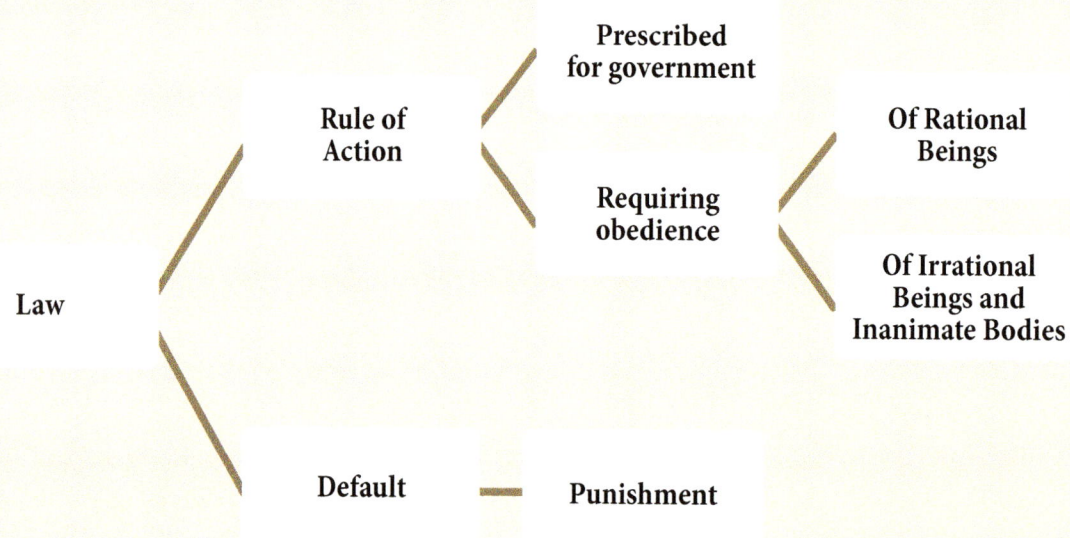

There are basically two types of law: natural law and revealed law. Revealed law is learned by study of the Word of God and prayer. Our Founders called this law the law of nature's God. Revealed law is the most authoritative as it is given directly by God.

"Laws of Nature and of Nature's God"

Mr. Ben Gilmore of Sacramento, California, a teacher of Christian history, has given us his excellent explanation of natural law and revealed law:

In the beginning, God ...

That is where everything that exists originates. Nothing exists without a set of rules to govern, i.e. direct, regulate, control, and restrain. We call these rules, "law." A law is a "rule of action."

In the 17th and 18th centuries (1600's & 1700's) literacy and the Bible in the common language were producing many scholars like Montesquieu, a French philosopher, and William Blackstone, "Father of the legal profession."

> *[Charles Montesquieu, born 1689] Laws in their most general signification, are the necessary relations arising from the nature of things. In this sense all beings have their laws: the Deity His laws, the material world its laws, the intelligences superior to man their laws, the beasts their laws, man his laws.*

Ponder – Write examples of "the Deity's laws", "the beasts their laws", "man his laws."

> *They who assert that a blind fatality produced the various effects we behold in this world talk very absurdly; for can anything be more unreasonable than to pretend that a blind fatality could be productive of intelligent beings?*

Ponder – What is "blind fatality"? What did Montesquieu think about "evolution?"

> *There is, then, a prime reason; and laws are the relations subsisting between it and different beings, and the relations of these to one another.*

Ponder – What is the "prime reason" for everything? Consider "intelligent design."

> *God is related to the universe, as Creator and Preserver; the laws by which He created all things are those by which He preserves them. He acts according to these rules, because He knows them; He knows them, because He made them; and He made them, because they are in relation of his Wisdom and power ...*[1]

> *[Sir William Blackstone, born 1723] Meaning of law.—Law, in its most general and comprehensive sense, signifies a <u>rule of action</u>; and is applied indiscriminately to all kinds of action, whether animate or inanimate, rational or irrational. Thus we say, the laws of motion, of gravitation, of optics, or mechanics, as well as the laws of nature and of nations. And it is that rule of action, which is prescribed by some superior, and which the inferior is bound to obey.*[2]

Ponder – Read the first paragraph from Montesquieu (above). Now reread what Blackstone has written. Next, note their life dates. Do you suppose Blackstone read Montesquieu?

---

[1] Hall, *CHOC I*, 134.
[2] Hall, *CHOC I*, 140.

🗨 *Ponder some more – What was your reaction when you read, "which the inferior is bound to obey."?*

America's founders recognized this in our "Declaration of Independence" –

> *"When in the Course of human events it becomes necessary for one people to dissolve the political bands which have connected them with another and to assume among the powers of the earth, the separate and equal station to which the <u>Laws of Nature and of Nature's God</u> entitle them, a decent respect to the opinions of mankind requires that they should declare the causes which impel them to the separation."*[3]

🗨 *Ponder – Notice two sets of laws?*

Let us look first at the "Laws of Nature" then at "The Laws of Nature's God."

THE LAWS OF NATURE

Sir William Blackstone continues:

> *"Thus when the Supreme Being formed the universe, and created matter out of nothing, He impressed certain principles upon that matter, from which it can never depart, and without which it would cease to be." Blackstone develops, step by step, the laws of motion and that things work well as long as they operate within those laws.*[4]

🗨 *Ponder – The "father of the legal profession" knew that the Supreme Being formed the universe!*

In his next paragraph, Blackstone points out that plants and animals are also governed, "by unerring rules laid down by the great Creator." After that he focuses upon,

> *… human action or conduct: that is, the precepts by which man, the noblest of all sublunary beings, a creature endowed with both reason and free will, is commanded to make use of those faculties in the general regulation of his behavior.*

[Sublunary, adj., Merely terrestrial, earthly, pertaining to this world.]

🗨 *Ponder – What is a "sublunary being?" Why is man the "noblest?" What are his "faculties?"*

Blackstone is about ready to define "Natural Law" –

> *Man, considered as a creature, must necessarily be subject to the laws of his Creator, for he is entirely a dependent being.*

🗨 *Ponder – How are you "entirely dependent" upon God?*

> *A being independent of any other, has no rule to pursue, but such as he prescribes to himself; but a state of dependence will inevitably oblige the inferior to take the will of him, on whom he depends, as the rule of his conduct; not indeed in every particular, but in all those points wherein his dependence consists.*

---

3 Hall, *CHOC I*, 346B.
4 Hall, *CHOC I*, 140.

Ponder – Have you ever heard, "If you live in my house you will obey the house rules!" This principle, therefore, has more or less extent and effect, in proportion as the superiority of the one and the dependence of the other is greater or less, absolute or limited. And consequently, as man depends absolutely upon his maker for everything, it is necessary that he should in all points conform to his Maker's will.[5]

> **Law of nature**—*This will of his Maker is called the law of nature. He created man, and endued him with free will to conduct himself in all parts of life, He laid down certain immutable laws of human nature, whereby that free will is in some degree regulated and restrained, and gave him also the faculty of reason to discover the purport of those laws.*

The Spirit of Laws

Ponder – How is your "free will" restrained, i.e. governed, by "laws of human nature?"

Blackstone goes on to point out that since God is all-powerful He could make whatever laws He pleased! But since He is also infinitely wise, He has made only such laws that are just.

Ponder – Why would it be unwise to make unjust laws? Does God conform to His laws?

> *… Such, among others, are these principles: that we should live honestly, should hurt nobody, and should render to everyone his due; to which three general precepts Justinian (a Byzantine emperor from 527 to 565) has reduced the whole doctrine of law.*

Ponder – What three principles summed up 6th century concepts of law?

The Laws of Nature's God

Blackstone called this set of laws, "Revealed Law."

> *"Revealed Law—This has given manifold occasion for the benign interposition of divine providence; which, in compassion to the frailty, the imperfection, and the blindness of human reason hath been pleased, at sundry times and in divers manners, to discover and enforce its laws by an immediate and direct revelation."[6]*

Interpretation – Because man neglected to reason it out on his own, many times it pleased God to step in and make it clear by direct revelation!

The doctrines thus delivered we call the <u>revealed or divine law</u>, and they are to be found only in the Holy Scriptures.

Ponder – Will Natural Law and Revealed Law ever be in conflict?

Natural laws are discovered by observation and reason. (Experience with fire quickly teaches a child not to touch fire.) But both human observation and human reason are imperfect. Once they thought the earth was flat because they could see the edge.

We <u>learn</u> revealed laws (The Bible) by study and prayer. Revealed Law (The Bible) has infinitely more

---

5 Hall, *CHOC I*, 141.
6 Hall, *CHOC I*, 142.

authority than Natural Law because it comes <u>directly from God</u> by dictation. Whereas, we discover Natural Law by imperfect observation and reason. If our human observation and reason were perfect, we wouldn't need the Bible. God is revealed in His creation.

Natural law and revealed law come from the same source and thus, will never be in conflict. If they appear to be in conflict, trust the Bible and recheck your observation and reason.

Ponder – How long did natural law exist before revealed law existed?

> **Emphatic Conclusion: Natural law is resident in the universe and in the human heart; God codified natural law in the Bible – the revealed law by which we best live.**

Copy the emphatic conclusion into your notebook.

Explain natural law and revealed law from your own understanding. List the key facts that describe natural law and revealed law on the following T chart in your notebook:

Natural Law	Revealed Law

Moral Law and the Preparation for Christ

Moral law: the law of God that prescribes the moral or social duties, and prohibits the transgression of them.

Revealed law is the written Word of God that came to us by God's design to make clear His moral governance of the world. It became necessary for the law to be given in written form and God chose a human instrument to deliver it.

The first major character that we shall consider in studying law is that of Moses, the first historian and the first lawgiver, whose contribution to mankind's effort to be properly governed is foundational. Through Moses we received the revealed law.

> **Now before faith came, we were held captive under the law, imprisoned until the coming faith would be revealed. Galatians 3:23**

The Ten Commandments—The Law[7]

"... these two tables recorded in the writings of Moses contain in a general form the vital principles of all modern legal science, judicial, national, and international. Is not that a fact upon scientific grounds worthy of careful study"? Rev. L.T. Townsend, *The Bible and Law*

"... 'When we consider attentively the institutions of Moses, we perceive that they comprehend every thing necessary for forming a civil establishment; not only precepts regarding the morals of the people, and the public and private offices of religion, but also laws of jurisprudence... I may add, they comprehend, also a sort of law of nations, for the use of that people, in adjusting the terms of their intercourse with other states and kingdoms, prescribing rules for the making and conducting of war and peace, entering into public treaties, and the like.'

"In Leviticus, Numbers and Deuteronomy, we have the ritual, moral, and civil law of the Jews." David Hoffman, *A Course of Legal Study*.

What does this selection say about the use of the Mosaic law?

Moses and the Law

The facts concerning Moses' deliverance of the Children of Israel from Egypt and God's revelation to him of the Ten Commandments may be found in *Exodus*, the second book of Moses, in the Holy Bible, chapters one through twenty. The account in the Bible is the primary source of this history.

There is an astounding story in God giving His holy law to all people. We will read a secondary source to fully appreciate the man Moses, his individuality, and how God prepared him to perform a most difficult task.

---

7 Slater, *T&L*, 158.

Moses, Hebrew Jurisprudence[8]

This interesting account of Moses is descriptive and imaginative while accurate to the Scripture.

"Among the great actors in the world's history must surely be presented the man who gave the first recorded impulse to civilization, and who is the most august character of antiquity. I think Moses and his legislation should be considered from the standpoint of the Scriptures rather than from that of science and criticism …

"Whether as a 'man of God,' or as a meditative sage, or as a sacred historian, or as an inspired prophet, or as an heroic liberator and leader of a favored nation, or as a profound and original legislator, Moses alike stands out as a wonderful man, not to the eyes of Jews merely, but to all enlightened nations and ages. He was evidently raised up for a remarkable and exalted mission,—not only to deliver a debased and superstitious people from bondage, but to impress mind and character upon them and upon all other nations, and to link his name with the progress of the human race.

The Decalogue…Hebrew Idea of Revealed Law

"He arose at a great crisis, when a new dynasty reigned in Egypt,—not friendly, as the preceding one had been, to the children of Israel; but a dynasty which had expelled the Shepherd Kings, and looked with fear and jealousy upon this alien race, already powerful, in sympathy with the old regime, located in the most fertile sections of the land, and acquainted not merely with agriculture, but with the arts of the Egyptians,—a population of over two millions of souls; so that the reigning monarch, probably a son of the Sesostris of the Greeks, bitterly exclaimed to his courtiers, 'The children of Israel are more and mightier than we!' And the consequence of this jealousy was a persecution based on the elemental principle of all persecution—that of fear blended with envy, carried out with remorseless severity; for in case of war (and the new dynasty scarcely felt secure on the throne) it was feared the Hebrews might side with enemies. So the new Pharaoh (Rameses II, as is thought by Rawlinson) attempted to crush their spirit by hard toils and unjust exactions. And as they still continued to multiply, there came forth the dreadful edict that every male child of the Hebrews should be destroyed as soon as born.

"It was then that Moses, descended from a family of the tribe of Levi, was born—1571 B.C., according to Usher. I need not relate in detail the beautiful story of his concealment for three months by his mother Jochebed, his exposure in a basket of papyrus on the banks of the Nile, his rescue by the daughter of Pharaoh, at that time regent of the kingdom in the absence of her father—or, as Wilberforce thinks, the wife of the king of Lower Egypt—his adoption by this powerful princess, his education in the royal household among those learned priests to whose caste even the King belonged. Moses himself, a great master of historical composition, has in six verses told that story, with singular pathos and beauty; yet he directly relates nothing further of his life until, at the age of forty, he killed an Egyptian overseer who was smiting one of his oppressed brethren, and buried him in the sands—thereby showing that he was indignant at injustice, or clung in his heart to his race of slaves.

---

8 John Lord, *Beacon Lights of History*, Vol. II (James Clarke & Co.,1888), 97–129.

"But what a history might have been written of those forty years of luxury, study, power, and honor!—since Josephus speaks of his successful and brilliant exploits as a conqueror of the Ethiopians. What a career did the son of the Hebrew bondwoman probably lead in the palaces of Memphis, sitting at the monarch's table, feted as a conqueror, adopted as grandson and perhaps as heir, a proficient in all the learning and arts of the most civilized nation of the earth, enrolled in the college of priests, discoursing with the most accomplished of his peers on the wonders of magical enchantment, the hidden meaning of religious rites, and even the being and attributes of a Supreme God,—the esoteric wisdom from which even a Pythagoras drew his inspiration; possibly tasting, with generals and nobles, all the pleasures of sin. But whether in pleasure or honor, the soul of Moses, fortified by the maternal instructions of his early days,—for his mother was doubtless a good as well as a brave woman, soars beyond his circumstances, and he seeks to avenge the wrongs of his brethren. Not wisely, however, for he slays a government official, and is forced to flee,—a necessity which we can hardly comprehend in view of his rank and power, unless it revealed all at once to the astonished king his Hebrew birth, and his dangerous sympathies with an oppressed people, the act showing that he may have sought, in his earnest soul, to break their intolerable bonds."

Write a T-chart and list the internal and external qualities of the character of Moses, "a wonderful man." Then continue reading:

Internal Qualities	External Qualities

Discuss: The upbringing and experiences of Moses were privileged; is it surprising that he would exhibit the leadership and allegiance to his Hebrew birth?

The continued reading of the story of Moses will be an exercise in how to best read primary and secondary sources of history that are often written in a language we might find challenging.

In this selection a <u>model of study</u> is provided that you will use in several other readings of the *Nation Makers* course. As you follow the exercise remember that you are learning a method of study of primary sources that will serve you well in your future studies.

Notice carefully the summary sentence that follows each paragraph 1-9. Do you think the suggested sentence summarizes the paragraph well? After paragraph 9, write your own one-sentence summary for each paragraph 10-15. You are practicing a sound method of study.

1. "Certainly Moses aspires prematurely to be a deliverer. He is not yet prepared for such a mighty task. He is too impulsive and inexperienced. It must need be that he pass through a period of preparation, learn patience, mature his knowledge, and gain moral force, which preparation could be best made in severe contemplation; for it is in retirement and study that great men forge the weapons which demolish principalities and powers, and master those principia which are the foundation of thrones and empires. So he retires to the deserts of Midian, among a scattered pastoral people, on the eastern shore of the Red Sea, and is received by Jethro, a priest of Midian, whose flocks he tends, and whose daughter he marries.

The child Moses on the Nile, Doré

Moses needed a period of preparation to be ready to accomplish the task God had for him.

2. "The land of Midian, to which he fled, is not fertile like Egypt, nor rich in unnumbered monuments of pride and splendor, with pyramids for mausoleums, and colossal statues to perpetuate kingly memories. It is not scented with flowers and variegated with landscapes of beauty and fertility, but is for the most part, with here and there a patch of verdure, a land of utter barrenness and dreariness, and, as Hamilton paints is, 'a great and terrible wilderness, where no soft features mitigated the unbroken horror, but dark and brown ridges, red peaks like pyramids of fire; no rounded hillocks or soft mountain curves, but monstrous and misshapen cliffs, rising tier above tier, and serrated for miles into rugged grandeur, and grooved by the winter torrents cutting into the veins of the fiery rock: a land dreary and desolate, yet sublime in its boldness and ruggedness,—a labyrinth of wild and blasted mountains, a terrific and howling desolation.'

His preparation was in a barren wilderness, "a howling desolation."

3. "It is here that Moses seeks safety, and finds it in the home of a priest, where his affections may be cultivated, and where he may indulge in lofty speculations and commune with the Elohim whom he adores; isolated yet social, active in body but more active in mind, still fresh in all the learning of the experiences of forty years. And the result of his studies and inspirations was, it is supposed, the book of Genesis, in which he narrates more important events, and reveals more lofty truths than all the historians of Greece unfolded in their collective volumes,—a marvel of historic art, a model of composition, an immortal work of genius, the oldest and the greatest written history of which we have record.

In this barren wilderness it is thought that Moses wrote Genesis.

4. "And surely what poetry, pathos, and eloquence, what simplicity and beauty, what rich and varied lessons of human experience, what treasures of moral wisdom, are revealed in that little book! How sublimely the poet prophet narrates the misery of the Fall, and the promised glories of the Restoration! How concisely the historian compresses the incidents of patriarchal life, the rise of empires, the fall of cities, the certitudes

of faith, of friendship, and of love! All that is vital in the history of thousands of years is condensed into a few chapters,—not dry and barren annals, but descriptions of character, and the unfolding of emotions and sensibilities, and insight into those principles of moral government which indicate a superintending Power, creating faith in a world of sin, and consolation amid the wreck of matter.

Genesis is a masterpiece of literature as well as a moral guide.

5. "Thus when forty more years are passed in study, in literary composition, in religious meditation, and active duties, in sight of grand and barren mountains, amid affections and simplicities,—years which must have familiarized him with every road and cattle-drive and sheep-track, every hill and peak, every wady and water-course, every timber-belt and oasis in the Sinaitic wilderness, through which his providentially trained military instincts were to safely conduct a vast multitude,—Moses, still strong and laborious, is fitted for his exalted mission as a deliverer. And now he is directly called by the voice of God himself, amid the wonders of the burning bush,—Him whom, thus far, he had, like Abraham, adored as the Elohim, the God Almighty, but whom henceforth he recognizes as Jehovah (Jahveh) in His special relations to the Jewish nation rather than as the general Deity who unites the attributes ascribed to Him as the ruler of the universe. Moses quakes before that awful voice out of the midst of the bush, which commissions him to deliver his brethren. He is no longer bold, impetuous, impatient, but timid and modest. Long study and retirement from the busy haunts of men have made him self-distrustful. He replies to the great I Am, 'Who am I, that I should bring forth the Children of Israel out of Egypt? Behold, I am not eloquent; they will not believe me, nor hearken to my voice.' In spite of the miracle of the rod, Moses obeys reluctantly, and Aaron, his elder brother, is appointed as his spokesman.

Moses is "fitted" and called to serve and is humbled by his calling.

6. "Armed with the mysterious wonder-working rod, at length Moses and Aaron, as representatives of the Jewish people, appear in the presence of Pharaoh, and in the name of Jehovah request permission for Israel to go and hold a feast in the wilderness. They do not demand emancipation or emigration, which would of course be denied. I cannot dwell on the haughty scepticism and obdurate hardness of the King,—'Who is Jehovah, that I should obey his voice?'—the renewed persecution of the Hebrews, the successive plagues and calamities sent upon Egypt, which the magicians could not explain, and the final extorted and unwilling consent of Pharaoh to permit Israel to worship the God of Moses in the wilderness, lest greater evils should befall him than the destruction of the first-born throughout the land.

Armed with the rod, he and Aaron request Pharaoh to release his people to perform a feast.

7. "The deliverance of a nation of slaves is at last, it would seem, miraculously effected; and then begins the third period of the life of Moses, as the leader and governor of these superstitious, sensual, idolatrous, degraded slaves. Then begin the real labors and trials of Moses; for the people murmur, and are consumed with fears as soon as they have crossed the sea, and find themselves in the wilderness....

Under great difficulty, Moses leads his people through the wilderness.

8. "But the distinguishing labor of Moses during these forty years, by which he linked his name with all subsequent ages, and became the greatest benefactor of mind the world has seen until Christ, was his system of Jurisprudence. It is this which especially demands our notice, and hence will form the main subject of this lecture.

His greatest achievement was delivering the Law of God to all people.

9. "In reviewing the Mosaic legislation, we notice both those ordinances which are based on immutable truth for the rule of all nations to the end of time, and those prescribed for the peculiar situation and exigencies of the Jews as a theocratic state, isolated from other nations.

Two types of ordinances were in the law: those for all nations always and those for the Jews alone.

Record the one-sentence summaries above of this account of Moses in your notebook. Continue 10-15 writing your own one-sentence summaries of each numbered paragraph.

10. "The moral code of Moses, by far the most important and universally accepted, rests on the fundamental principles of theology and morality. How lofty, how impressive, how solemn this code! How it appeals at once to the consciousness of all minds in every age and nation, producing convictions that no sophistry can weaken, binding the conscience with irresistible and terrific bonds,—those immortal Ten Commandments, engraved on the two tables of stone, and preserved in the holy and innermost sanctuary of the Jews, yet reappearing in all their literature, accepted and reaffirmed by Christ, entering into the religious system of every nation that has received them, and forming the cardinal principles of all theological belief! Yet it was by Moses that these Commandments came. He is the first, the favored man, commissioned by God to declare to the world, clearly and authoritatively, His supreme power and majesty, whom alone all nations and tribes and people are to worship to remotest generations....

11. "All Christian nations have accepted these Ten Commandments, even Mohammedan nations, as appealing to the universal conscience,—not a mere Jewish code, but primary law, susceptible of boundless obligation, never to be abrogated; a direct injunction of the Almighty to the end of time.

12. "The Ten Commandments seem to be the foundation of the subsequent and more minute code which Moses gave to the Jews; and it is interesting to see how its great principles have entered, more or less, into the laws of Christian nations from the decline of the Roman Empire, into the Theodosian code, the laws of Charlemagne, of Ina, of Alfred, and especially into the institutions of the Puritans, and of all other sects and parties wherever the Bible is studied and revered.... Moses, from first to last, insists imperatively on the doctrine of personal responsibility to God, which doctrine is the logical sequence of belief in Him as the moral governor of the world. And in enforcing this cardinal truth he is dogmatic and dictatorial, as a prophet and ambassador of the Most High should be....

13. "The other laws which Moses promulgated are more special and minute, and seem to be intended to preserve the Jews from idolatry, the peculiar sin of the surrounding nations; and also, more directly, to keep alive the recognition of a theocratic government.

14. "Thus the ceremonial or ritualistic law—an important part of the Mosaic Code—constantly points to Jehovah as the King of the Jews, as well as their Supreme Deity, for whose worship the rites and ceremonies are devised with great minuteness, to keep His *personality* constantly before their minds. Moreover, all their rites and ceremonies were typical and emblematical of the promised Savior who was to arise; in a more emphatic sense their King, and not merely their own Messiah, but the Redeemer of the whole race, who should reign finally as King of kings and Lord of lords. And hence these rites and sacrifices, typical of Him who should offer Himself as a sacrifice for the sins of the world, are not supposed to be binding on other nations after the great sacrifice has been made, and the law of Moses has been fulfilled by Jesus and the new dispensation has been established….

15. "Thus did Moses, instructed by God,—for this is the great fact revealed in his testimony, lead the inconstant Israelites through a forty years' pilgrimage, securing their veneration to the last. Thus did he keep them from the idolatries for which they hankered, and preserved among them allegiance to an invisible King. Thus did he impress his own mind and character upon them, and shape their institutions with matchless wisdom. Thus did he give them a system of laws—moral, ceremonial, and civil—which kept them a powerful and peculiar people for more than a thousand years, and secured a prosperity which culminated in the glorious reigns of David and Solomon and a political power unsurpassed in Western Asia, to see which the Queen of Sheba came from the uttermost part of the earth,—nay, more, which first formulated for that little corner of the world principles and precepts concerning the relations of men to God and to one another which have been an inspiration to all mankind for thousands of years."

Civil Law and Nation Making

Preparation for Christianity: Israel, Greece, and Rome

Many links were forged on Christianity's Chain as it moved westward. The non-Christian historian reading history often mistakes the contributions from the past and overlooks those links that forwarded Christianity. Let us look at two nations that often are regarded as furnishing Americans with blueprints for our own form of government. After you have studied the character and government of these two nations perhaps you will see why it depends upon your philosophy of history and of government—your point of view—as to how you will interpret the events of history.

The Pagan Elements in History

We cannot study American and Western Civilization without becoming aware of the presence of a heritage from Greece and from Rome. There are those today that claim that our institutions of government, our architecture, our city plans, our sciences, and our literature, all reflect our debt to a pagan past. They point to many external symbols remaining with us in order to trace the lineage of our beginnings.

For the Christian there is the recognition that God is the Disposer of men and nations. Thus God assigned to each nation a special role to play, contributions to make, and all of these "separate stones and pillars" became building blocks to be used by "the Master Builder" as the Chain of Christianity® moved westward to America.

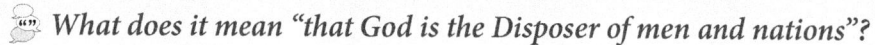 *What does it mean "that God is the Disposer of men and nations"?*

If we remember that "the glory that was Greece, and the grandeur that was Rome" have vanished—to remain only as emblems of a pagan past—we can see how God might use aspects from these nations to be recast by the Christians of our nations—fashioned anew for His purpose. Charles Bancroft in tracing the contributions of past civilizations before they reached America stated,

> *All the past has contributed to the excellence of her foundation and modern Europe has supplied her with the most desirable building material both of ideas and of men. Without Asia, Greece, and Rome, there would have been a very imperfect modern Europe; and without modern Europe, America must have begun at the beginning, with all the lessons, discoveries and discipline of thousands of years to learn.*[9]

The Christian scholar admits the presence of the pagan elements in our national heritage, but he recognizes that without Christianity these elements would not have been found useful. Like the pillars of the Parthenon or the Acropolis in Athens, or the seats in the crumbling Coliseum in Rome, they would lie in the dust of the ages—monuments to a dead past. But with the quickening spirit of the Gospel's westward move, the best elements of the pagan past were utilized, particularly in America where the liberty of the individual could choose to use what served best to embellish the "grand Temple of Civilization." Thus the Founding Father generations utilized the marble columned buildings to suggest dignity and order as they constructed the new capitol of the nation in Washington on the Potomac River. Many of the homes of the New Republic—the world's first Christian Republic—utilized classical architecture to express the beauty of Christian Constitutional liberty.

What is the role of the past in furnishing the present? Explain the use of much of the pagan past to the forming of a new nation in America.

---

[9] Hall, *CHOC I*, 9.

God Uses Three Nations

"The three great historical nations had to contribute, each in its own peculiar way, to prepare the soil for the planting of Christianity,—the Jews on the side of the religious element; the Greeks on the side of science and art; the Romans, as masters of the world, on the side of the political element. When the fullness of time was arrived, and Christ appeared,—when the goal of history had thus been reached,—then it was, that through Him, and by the power of the spirit that proceeded from Him,—the might of Christianity,—all the threads, hitherto separated, of human development, were to be brought together and interwoven in one web."[10]

Greece—A Language for the New Testament

"If we think of the civilization of the Greeks, we have no difficulty in fixing on its chief characteristics… We have only to do with this national character so far as, under divine Providence, it was made subservient to the spread of the Gospel.

"We shall see how remarkably it served this purpose, if we consider the tendency of the Greeks to trade and colonization.… To all these places they carried their arts and literature, their philosophy, their mythology, and their amusement. They carried also their arms and their trade.

"Of all the Greek elements … the spread of the language is the most important. That language, which is the richest and most delicate that the world has seen, became the language of theology. The Greek tongue became to the Christian more than it had been to the Roman or the Jew.… It was not an accident that the New Testament was written in Greek, the language which can best express the highest thoughts and worthiest feelings of the intellect and heart.…"[11]

Rome—A United World Empire

"The idea of law had grown up with the growth of the Romans; and wherever they went they carried it with them. Wherever their armies were marching or encamping, there always attended them, like a mysterious presence, the spirit of the city of Rome. Universal conquest and permanent occupation were the ends at which they aimed.… It is easy to see how much misery followed in the train of Rome's advancing greatness. Cruel suffering was a characteristic feature of the close of the republic…

"It should be remembered, in the first place, that the Romans had already become Greek to some considerable extent, before they were the political masters of those eastern countries, where the language, mythology, and literature of Greece had become more or less familiar.… Is it too much to say, that the general Latin conquest was providentially delayed till the Romans had been sufficiently imbued with the language and ideas of their predecessors, and had incorporated many parts of that civilization with their own?

"And if the wisdom of the divine pre-arrangements is illustrated by the period of the spread of the Greek language, it is illustrated no less by that of the completion and maturity of the Roman government. When all parts of the civilized world were bound together in one empire,—when one common organization pervaded the whole,—when channels of communication were everywhere opened—when new facilities of travelling were provided,—then was 'the fullness of time' (Gal. 4:4), then the Messiah came. The Greek language had already been prepared as a medium for preserving and transmitting the doctrine; the Roman government was now prepared to help the progress even of that religion which it persecuted. The manner in which it spread through the provinces is well exemplified in the life of St. Paul; his right of citizenship rescued him in

---

10 Slater, T&L, 160.
11 Slater, T&L, 162.

Judea and in Macedonia; he converted one governor in Cyprus, was protected by another in Achaia, and was sent from Jerusalem to Rome by a third. The time was approaching, when all the complicated weight of the central tyranny and of the provincial governments, was to fall on the new and irresistible religion. But before this took place, it had begun to grow up in close connection with all departments of the Empire."[12]

Salvation is of the Jews

"In Judaism the true religion is prepared for man; in heathenism man is prepared for the true religion. The heathen preparation was partly intellectual and literary, as represented by the Greeks; and partly political and social as represented by the Romans. Jerusalem becomes the Holy City, Athens the city of culture, and Rome the city of power—all three factors find their answer and fulfillment in Christ.

"Judaism is in sharp contrast with the idolatrous nations of antiquity—it was like an oasis in a desert, clearly defined and isolated; separated and enclosed by a rigid moral and ceremonial law. The Holy Land itself, though in the midst of the three Continents of the ancient world, and surrounded by the great nations, was separated from them by deserts south and east, by sea on the west, and by mountains on the north; thus securing to the Mosaic religion freedom to unfold itself and to fulfill its great work without disturbing influences. God was particular about his geographical arrangements."[13]

How does God use each of the three great historical nations to prepare the soil for the planting of Christianity?

Write a chart to record the contributions of each of the three nations to the coming of Christ:

Greece	Rome	Hebrew

A Study of Contrasting Influences: Pagan & Christian

When our Lord taught, he frequently used contrast as a means of heightening the appeal of the distinctly Christian idea of man and government—the flow of force and power in an individual's life. In Jesus' "Parable of the Sower," we read of three types of soil or character: the barren wayside, the stony ground, and the thorns, all contrasted with the "good ground." In the "Parable of the Two Foundations," one house was built upon sand, one on rock, with the evident result when the "rain descended, and the floods came, and the winds blew." While these parables refer to the life of the believer, they afford excellent examples of the use of contrast in teaching.

---

12 Slater, *T&L*, 162-165.
13 V.M. Hall, "Lectures in History" (unpublished).

So as we become aware of the world of pagan mythology and idolatry, especially in the study of the Greeks and the Romans, we recognize their pervasive influence still in our world today. Therefore it is necessary to identify to our students and our children, a contrast of foundations between the "Rock of our salvation"— Jesus Christ, and the sandy shifting foundations, upon which these make-believe deities are based. Moreover, since it is the nature of mythology to assume many faces, it is important for our students to see the clear-cut contrasts between the world of the pagan, past or present, and the redeemed life of the believer.

The Contrast Between Christianity and Paganism

The Murder of Cicero

"Christianity could not have taken a firm hold on human nature, if it had not penetrated it by its divine power, and thus verified itself to be indeed that which alone can satisfy the higher necessities of the inner man. This divine power of the gospel revealed itself to the heathen in the lives of Christians, which showed forth the virtues of him who had called them out of darkness into his marvelous light, and enabled them to walk as the children of God, in the midst of a perverse generation, among whom they shone as lights in the world....

"They saw Christians meet death in the confidence of their faith with the greatest firmness and cheerfulness, oftentimes amidst extreme tortures ... Many asked, what gives men such energy to do and suffer everything on account of their convictions, in an age of such abject weakness, when we see all things bending before earthly power? Whoever proposed this question endeavoured to make himself acquainted with Christianity; and the consequence was, that the inquirer became captivated with the divine doctrine."[14]

THERE IS NONE RIGHTEOUS, NO NOT ONE: THERE IS NONE THAT UNDERSTANDETH, THERE IS NONE THAT SEEKETH AFTER GOD. FOR ALL HAVE SINNED, AND COME SHORT OF THE GLORY OF GOD... ROMANS 3:10–11, 23

FOR THE WAGES OF SIN IS DEATH; BUT THE GIFT OF GOD IS ETERNAL LIFE THROUGH JESUS CHRIST OUR LORD.
ROMANS 6:23

---

14 Slater, *T&L*, 210.

> AND THIS IS THE RECORD, THAT GOD HATH GIVEN TO US ETERNAL LIFE,
> AND THIS LIFE IS IN HIS SON. HE THAT HATH THE SON HATH LIFE;
> AND HE THAT HATH NOT THE SON OF GOD HATH NOT LIFE. 1 JOHN 5:11–12

"The Bible is the only source of man's knowledge of how to obtain and maintain Christian civil liberty, and history shows that according to the degree the Bible has been received by the individual and its contents related to all aspects of his life, has Christian civil freedom risen or declined.

"To learn of salvation through Jesus Christ, and how to live the Christian life, the Bible must be opened to the individual. Therefore the *history of the Bible* in the hands of the individual is the *history of Christian civil government*. Also, because the church is the assembly or congregation of believers, whatever is reasoned from Scripture regarding church polity or government, is the precursor of civil polity or government. Thus it also can be said that the *history of church government* is the *history of Christian civil government*."[15]

Emphatic Conclusion: "Almost all the civil liberty now enjoyed in the world owes its origin to the principles of the Christian religion. Men began to understand their natural rights, as soon as the reformation from popery began to dawn in the sixteenth century; and civil liberty has been gradually advancing and improving as genuine Christianity has prevailed."[16]

Discuss the relationship of Christianity to civil liberty.

Copy the emphatic conclusion in your notebook.

Christianity–The Gospel

Neander's discussion of the individualities of national character of the Greeks and the Romans:[17]

Christianity alone brings true liberty and it establishes as the basis of government—the Christian idea of man. The Gospel brings forth a higher standard of liberty than *external law*—rather that *internal law* of the Two Commandments of our Lord. Christianity's government is self-government—and he that accepts the Gospel is willing "to bring into captivity every thought to the obedience of Christ" (2 Cor. 10:5).

For centuries men sought freedom from slavery and tyranny. They believed their liberation to be dependent upon *external* circumstances. But it was not until the Saviour of mankind appeared that men learned that external freedom was achieved by internal liberty—"the liberty wherewith Christ hath made us free" [J.H. Merle D'Aubigne, D.D., *History of the Reformation in Europe*].

"The greatest and most dangerous of despotisms is that beneath which the depraved inclination of human nature, the deadly influence of the world, namely, sin, miserably subjects the human conscience. There are, no doubt many countries, especially among those which the sun of Christianity has not yet illumined, that

---

15 V.M. Hall, *The Christian History of the American Revolution: Consider and Ponder* (FACE, 1976), XXIV.
16 Noah Webster, *History of the United States*, (Durrie & Peck, 1833), 273.
17 Slater, *T&L*, 159.

are without civil liberty, and that groan under the arbitrary rule of powerful masters. But, in order to become free outwardly, men must first succeed in being free inwardly. In the human heart there is a vast country to be delivered from slavery—abysses which man cannot cross alone, heights he cannot climb unaided, fortresses he cannot take, armies he cannot put to flight. In order to conquer in this moral battle, man must unite with One stronger than himself—with the Son of God."

Christianity moved Westward—each move bringing forth the evidence that freedom and progress for man rests only with the achievement of spiritual liberty—"the glorious liberty of the children of God" (Rom. 8:21). Thus the Christian idea of man and government had to take shape through the centuries as men grasped the idea of Christian self-government.

Discuss the contrast of Christianity and paganism and summarize why Christianity alone brings liberty.

Nation Making by Slavery—Greek Democracy[18]

"When we contemplate Greece, and especially when we fix our eyes on Athens, our admiration is strongly, I had almost said, is irresistibly excited, in reflecting, that such a diminutive spot concentrated within itself whatever is great and eminent in almost every point of view; whatever confers distinction on the human intellect; whatever is calculated to inspire wonder, or communicate delight. Athens was the pure well-head of poetry:

> 'HITHER, AS TO THEIR FOUNTAIN, OTHER STARS
>
> REPAIRING, IN THEIR GOLDEN URNS DRAW LIGHT.'

> "IT WAS THE THEATRE OF ARMS, THE CRADLE OF THE ARTS, THE
> SCHOOL OF PHILOSOPHY, AND THE PARENT OF ELOQUENCE."

"To be regarded as the masters in learning, the oracle of taste, and the standard of politeness, to the whole civilized world, is a splendid distinction. But it is a pestilent mischief, when the very renown attending such brilliant advantages becomes the vehicle for carrying into other countries the depraved manners by which these pre-eminent advantages are accompanied. This was confessedly the case of Greece with respect to Rome. Rome had conquered Greece by her arms; but whenever a subjugated country contributes, <u>by her vices, to enslave the state which conquered her, she amply revenges herself</u> …

"Many of the Athenian vices originated in the very nature of their constitution; in the very spirit of that turbulent democracy which Solon could not restrain, nor the ablest of his successors control …

"This unsettled government, which left the country perpetually exposed to the tyranny of the few, and the turbulence of the many, was never bound together by any principle of union, by any bond of interest, common to the whole community, except when the general danger, for a time, annihilated the distinction of separate interests. The restraint of laws was feeble; the laws themselves were often contradictory; often ill administered; popular intrigues, and tumultuous assemblies, frequently obstructing their operation …

"By this light and capricious people, acute in their feelings, carried away by every sudden gust of passion,

---

18 Slater, *T&L*, 160-162.

Homer Reciting the Iliad

as mutable in their opinions as unjust in their decisions, the most illustrious patriots were first sacrificed, and then honored with statues; their heroes were murdered as traitors, and then reverenced as gods …

"We shall see how remarkably it subserved this purpose, if we consider the tendency of the Greeks to trade and colonization. Their mental activity was accompanied with great physical restlessness. This clever people always exhibited a disposition to spread themselves.… At the earliest period at which history enables us to discover them, we see them moving about in their ships on the shores and among the islands of their native seas; and three or four centuries before the Christian era, Asia Minor, beyond which the Persians had not been permitted to advance, was bordered by a fringe of Greek colonies … To all these places they carried their arts and literature, their philosophy, their mythology, and their amusement. They carried also their arms and their trade …

"Of all the Greek elements … the spread of the language is the most important. That language, which is the richest and most delicate that the world has seen, became the language of theology. The Greek tongue became to the Christian more than it had been to the Roman or the Jew.… It was not an accident that the New Testament was written in Greek, the language which can best express the highest thoughts and worthiest feelings of the intellect and heart, and which is adapted to be the instrument of education for all nations: nor was it an accident that the composition of these books and the promulgation of the Gospel were delayed, till the instruction of our Lord, and the writings of His Apostles, could be expressed in the dialect of Alexandria. This, also, must be ascribed to the foreknowledge of Him, who 'winked at the times of ignorance,' but who 'made of one blood all nations of men for to dwell on all the face of the earth, and determined the times before appointed and the bounds of their habitation [Revs. W. Conybeare and J.S. Howson, *The Life and Epistles of St. Paul*].'"

How did Rome conquer Greece? How did Greece enslave Rome, her conqueror?

What form of government resulted in Greece as a result of her vices?

Be sure you understand the definitions of democracy, republic and tyranny.

DEMOC´RACY, n. [Gr. δημοκρατια; δημος, *people, and* κρατεω, *to possess, to govern*].

Government by the people; a form of government, in which the supreme power is lodged in the hands of the people collectively, or in which the people exercise the powers of legislation.

REPUB´LIC, n. [L. respublica; res *and* publica; *public affairs*].

A commonwealth; a state in which the exercise of the sovereign power is lodged in representatives elected by the people.

TYR´ANNY, n. [Fr. tyrannie; from tyran].

Arbitrary or despotic exercise of power; the exercise of power over subjects and others with a rigor not authorized by law or justice, or not requisite for the purposes of government. Hence tyranny is often synonymous with cruelty and oppression.

Can you see what key point distinguishes a republic from a democracy? Can either a republic or a democracy be a tyranny? What is America—a republic or a democracy? Why?

What great contribution did the Greeks make to mankind that only the Christian historian could appreciate?

Centralization Through Law—Roman Republic[19]

What key word do we associate with the Romans? How did Rome achieve her pre-eminence?

Write a one-sentence summary for each of the numbered paragraphs:

1. We have seen how the Greek science and commerce were wafted, by irregular winds, from coast to coast; and now we follow the advance of legions, governors, and judges along the Roman Roads, which pursued their undeviating course over plains and mountains, and bound the City to the furthest extremities of the provinces. "There is no better way of obtaining a clear view of the features and a correct idea of the spirit of the Roman age, than by considering the material works which still remain as its imperishable monuments. Whether undertaken by the hands of the government, or for the ostentation of private luxury, they were marked by vast extent and accomplished at an enormous expenditure. The gigantic roads of the empire have been unrivalled till the present century. Solid structures of all kinds, for utility, amusement and worship, were erected in Italy and the provinces, amphitheatres of stone, magnificent harbours, bridges, sepulchres, and temples . . .

2. "The statues, with which the metropolis and the Roman houses were profusely decorated, had been brought from plundered provinces, and many of them had swelled the triumphs of conquerors on the Capitol. The amphitheatres were built for shows of gladiators, and were the scenes of a bloody cruelty, which had been quite unknown in the licentious exhibitions of the Greek theatre. The roads, baths, harbours, aqueducts, had been constructed by slave-labour. And the country-villas, which the Italian traveller lingered to admire, were themselves vast establishments of slaves.

3. "It is easy to see how much misery followed in the train of Rome's advancing greatness. Cruel suffering was a characteristic feature of the close of the republic. Slave wars, civil wars, wars of conquest, had left their disastrous results behind them. No country recovers rapidly from the effects of a war which had been conducted within its frontier; and there was no district of the empire which had not been the scene of some recent campaign. None had suffered more than Italy itself [Revs. W. Conybeare and J.S. Howson, *The Life and Epistles of St. Paul*].

4. "'As regards the manners and mode of life of the Romans, their great object at this time was the acquisition and possession of money. Their moral conduct, which had been corrupt enough before the social war, became still more so by their systematic plunder and rapine. Immense riches were accumulated and squandered upon brutal pleasures …' [Niebuhr's *Lectures on the History of Rome.*]

---

19 Slater, *T&L*, 162-166.

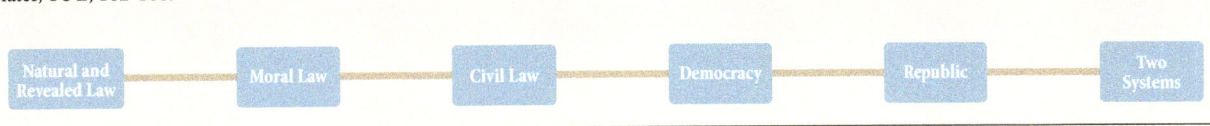

Part III: The Nature of Law

Arch of Constantine

5. "The Empire was only the order of external government, with a chaos both of opinions and morals within … The old severity of manners, and the old faith in the better part of the Roman religion, were gone. The licentious creeds and practices of Greece and the East had inundated Italy and the West; and the Pantheon was only the monument of a compromise among a multitude of effete superstitions. It is true that a remarkable religious toleration was produced by this state of things; and it is probable that for some short time Christianity itself shared the advantage of it. But still the temper of the times was essentially both cruel and profane; and the Apostles were soon exposed to its bitter persecutions. The Roman Empire was destitute of that unity which the Gospel gives to mankind. It was a kingdom of this world; and the human race was groaning for the better peace of 'a kingdom not of this world.'

6. "Thus in the very condition of the Roman Empire, and the miserable state of its mixed population, we can recognize a negative preparation for the Gospel of Christ. This tyranny and oppression called for a Consoler, as much as the moral sickness of the Greeks called for a Healer: a Messiah was needed by the whole Empire as much as by the Jews, though not looked for with the same conscious expectation. But we have no difficulty in going much farther than this, and we cannot hesitate to discover in the circumstances of the world at this period, significant traces of a positive preparation for the Gospel.

7. "And if the wisdom or the divine pre-arrangements is illustrated by the period of the spread of the Greek language, it is illustrated no less by that of the completion and maturity of the Roman government. When all parts of the civilized world were bound together in one empire,—when one common organization pervaded the whole,—when channels of communication were everywhere opened— when new facilities of travelling were provided,—then was 'the fullness of time' (Gal. 4:4), then the Messiah came. The Greek language had already been prepared as a medium for preserving and transmitting the doctrine; the Roman government was now prepared to help the progress even of that religion which it persecuted. The manner in which it spread through the provinces is well exemplified in the life of St. Paul; his right of citizenship rescued him in Judea and in Macedonia; he converted one governor in Cyprus, was protected by another in Achaia, and was sent from Jerusalem to Rome by a third. The time was indeed approaching, when all the complicated weight of the central tyranny, and of the provincial governments, was to fall on the new and irresistible religion. But before this took place, it had begun to grow up in close connection with all departments of the Empire [Niebuhr's *Lectures on the History of Rome*]."

Roman Civil Law

8. "Of the two chief systems of law in the world of today one, the modern Roman or civil law, is characteristically judicial. In antiquity, while originally the ultimate lawmaking power was theoretically in the Roman people, the Roman law grew chiefly through the edicts of the magistrates, and the writings of the juris-consults … In legal theory the emperor was the first citizen of Rome to whom the whole power of all the magistrates had been delegated by a statute. Thus the theory of the legal order was administrative …

"Whereas in the final Roman theory law proceeded from the emperor—was made by him—in the English theory it was pre-existing and was found by the king or by his justices and applied to the cases before them as something binding on them no less than on the parties.

> "As a result of this difference of attitude towards the law, the one system thinking of it as wholly the product of the government, the other thinking of a fundamental law binding the agencies of government, there is a characteristic difference as to declaration of rights and guarantees of liberties in the two systems [Roscoe Pound, *The Development of Constitutional Guarantees of Liberty*]."

Render therefore unto Caesar the things that are Caesar's; and unto God the things that are God's. Matthew 22:21

Render therefore to all their dues: tribute to whom tribute is due; custom to whom custom; fear to whom fear; honour to whom honour. Romans 13:7

Rome is often called the "master-builder" of the ancient world. Name some of the distinctive contributions of the Roman builders.

Did the Roman concentration of power and wealth bring happiness to all?

The Roman Empire is an example of one world under a one-world or centralized government. What held it together? What did it lack?

How did God use the one world of the Roman Empire to help Christianity?

We can refer to the government of Rome as government from the "top down." It was rule by the aristocracy. There was no such thing as "consent of the governed." American government markedly differs from the Roman republic in that the people elect their representatives.

The Greek city-states were small republics who often fought each other and found it difficult to unite against the external attack of an enemy.

What essential ingredient was lacking to unite these pagan republics?

In what nation does the representative principle become firmly established?

Define REPRESENT´, v. t. s as z. [Fr. representer; L. repræsento; re and Low L. præsento, from præsens, present.] To supply the place of; to act as a substitute for another. The parliament of Great Britain represents the nation. The congress of the United States represents the people or nation. The senate is considered as representing the states in their corporate capacity.

Natural and Revealed Law — Moral Law — Civil Law — Democracy — Republic — Two Systems

Part III: The Nature of Law

Representation in America

In America the idea of representative government derived its roots from the Bible and thus furnishes the purest standard to the world. A look at the first account of a written constitution in America is instructive as you examine the principles upon which it is based. Identify those principles for discussion as you read the following:

THE FIRST AMERICAN CONSTITUTION: 1638[20]

Fundamental Orders of Connecticut: Three Self-Governing Independent Connecticut Towns Form and Establish the First Written Constitution

… The same year, 1638, witnessed the preliminary proceedings, very imperfectly recorded, of one of the most interesting events in all civil history—the establishment of a written constitution for the government of the Colony; the "first written constitution," it has been called, "in the history of nations."

The common affairs of these towns along the River had at first been conducted by a provisional government under Massachusetts authority. But the term of that commission having expired, a General Court of the towns took its place. At some time in 1638 a General Court was elected for the purpose of framing a body of laws for the permanent government of the Colony. The deliberations of the assembly thus chosen have perished. We know only the result, which arrived at the authority of Fundamental Laws on the 14th of January, 1639.

That Charter of public rule was a document far in advance of anything the world had ever seen, in its recognition of the origin of all civil authority as derived, under God, from the agreement and covenant of the whole body of the governed. Such a "combination and Confederation together … to be guided and governed according to such Lawes, Rules, Orders, and decrees as shall be made, ordered & decreed," marks a reckoning point in the history and science of government.

But the chief interest in this matter, so far as the present chronicle is concerned, is not a scientific one, or even a historic one, reckoned from the point of the concerns of civil administration only. The interest of the subject, as connected with this Church survey, now in hand, is twofold: It is, first, that <u>the form of civil government here established was simply an extension to the domain of secular affairs of the principles already adopted in religious matters—the mutual covenant and agreement of those associated, as under God the ultimate law.</u> And, second, and more particularly, because of the agency in leading on to the establishment of this principle in the Fundamental Laws of this Colony, of <u>the wise and far-sighted Pastor of this Church.</u> We are indebted for the discovery of definite evidence of this agency—though it might have been antecedently conjectured from all that we know of the man who exercised it—to the skill and research of the distinguished antiquarian scholar, J. H. Trumbull. The evidence lay undiscovered more than two and a quarter centuries in a little, almost undecipherable volume of manuscript, written by a young man—Mr. Henry Wolcott, Jr., born January, 1610—in the neighbor town of Windsor. The volume contains notes in cipher of sermons and lectures preached by Rev. Messrs. Warham and Huit of Windsor, and Rev. Messrs. Hooker and Stone of Hartford. In it is found an abstract of Mr. Hooker's lecture given on "Thursday, May 31, 1638, at an adjourned session, probably of the April Court; and apparently designed to lead the way to the general recognition of the great truths which were soon to be successfully incorporated in the Fundamental Laws." The following is the deciphered abstract of the sermon:

Text: Deuteronomy 1:13. "Take you wise men, and understanding, and known among your tribes, and I will make them rulers over you." Captains over thousands, and captains over hundreds—over fifties—over tens, etc.

Doctrine. I. That the choice of public magistrates belongs unto the people by God's own allowance.

II. The privilege of election which belongs unto the people, therefore, must not be exercised according to

---

20 Hall, *CHOC* I, 249–252.

their humors, but according to the blessed will and law of God.

III. They who have power to appoint officers and magistrates, it is their power, also, to set the bounds of the power and place unto which they call them.

Reasons. I. Because the foundation of authority is laid, firstly, in the free consent of the people.

2. Because, by a free choice the hearts of the people will be more inclined to the love of the persons [chosen], and more ready to yield [obedience].

3. Because of that duty and engagement of the people.

Uses. The lesson taught is threefold:—

Ist. There is matter of thankful acknowledgment in the (appreciation) of God's faithfulness towards us and the permission of these measures that God doth commend and vouchsafe.

2ndly. Of reproof—to dash the conceits of all those that shall oppose it.

3rdly. Of exhortation—to persuade us as God hath given us liberty, to *take* it.

And lastly. As God hath spared our lives, and given us them in liberty, so to seek the guidance of God, and to choose in God and for God.

The doctrine was adapted to the auditors and to the time. It was harmonious with the experiences and the teachings of Providence in which the hearers had been led. But its statement was a novelty in politics, not the less. Dr. Bacon says of it: "That sermon by Thomas Hooker* from the pulpit of the First Church in Hartford, is the earliest known suggestion of a fundamental law, enacted not by royal charter, nor by concession from any previously existing government, but by the people themselves—a primary and supreme law by which the government is constituted, and which not only provides for the free choice of magistrates by the people, but also 'sets the bounds and limitations of the power and place to which' each magistrate is called."

Eight months later, the fundamental laws embodying these principles for the first time in human history, were "sentenced, ordered, and decreed." It is impossible not to recognize the Master hand. The Pastor of the Hartford Church was Connecticut's great Legislator, also.

[George Leon Walker, *History of the First Church in Hartford, 1633–1883*, Hartford, CT: Brown and Gross, 1884, 103–105]

What minister gave the sermon that brought forth the extension of Christianity to the civil sphere?

What was his Scriptural documentation for "representation"?

Where should Americans look for their standard of character?

Two Systems of Law: Roman and Common

There are two systems of law referred to here—the first, the **Roman system of law**—"social control through law." Civil Law, or that law which stems from the Roman system is law "written down" and which endeavors to spell out every detail and cover every situation. It is evident today in our lengthy Civil Codes governing many areas of life, such as our municipal codes dealing with building, sanitation, traffic, etc.

The other system of law refers to "unwritten law" or **Common Law**—law derived from custom or usage. English Common Law was first collected together and written down by William Blackstone in 1765. Common Law was considered to be derived from the Law of Nature. Noah Webster's 1828 *Dictionary* describes the Law of Nature as "a rule of conduct arising out of the natural relations of human beings established by the Creator, and existing prior to any positive precept."

John Locke further defines the Law of Nature as God's Law.[21]

6. "But though this be a *State of Liberty*, yet it is not a *State of License*: though Man in that State have an uncontrolable Liberty to dispose of his person or possessions, yet he has not liberty to destroy himself, or so much as any creature in his possession, but where some nobler use than its bare preservation calls for it. The state of nature has a law of nature to govern it, which obliges every one: and reason, which is that law, teaches all mankind, who will but consult it, that being all *equal and independent*, no one ought to harm another in his life, health, liberty, or possessions: for men being all the workmanship of one omnipotent, and infinitely wise maker; all the servants of one sovereign master, sent into the world by his order, and about his business; they are his property, whose workmanship they are, made to last during his, not one another's pleasure: and being furnished with like faculties, sharing all in one community of nature, there cannot be supposed any such *subordination* among us, that may authorize us to destroy one another, as if we were made for one another's uses, as the inferior ranks of creatures are for our's. Every one, as he is *bound to preserve himself*, and not to quit his station willfully, so by the like reason, when his own preservation comes not in competition, ought he, as much as he can, *to preserve the rest of mankind*, and may not, unless it be to do justice on an offender, take away, or impair the life, or what tends to the preservation of the life, the liberty, health, limb, or goods of another."

In the Roman system of law who made the law? Did the law-maker in the Roman system have to abide by the law, or was he "above the law"?

In the English system, what was the Common Law found to be? Who was it binding on as well as on the people?

American Constitutional law is an outgrowth of English Common Law. There is only one American state where Roman Civil Law has played some part because of the influence of the French in its establishment. Do you know which one it is?

In essence, Common Law derives from the *internal* or Christian Law. Roman or Civil Law is that *external* law or control which originated in the world's greatest pagan nation.

When America has been at the peak of her Christian commitment, would there be more or less of external civil law in evidence? Why?

Today there is less and less evidence of internal Christian self-government in the life of the individual, and more and more external control by what? Is this trend good? Explain.

---

21 Hall, *CHOC I*, 58.

Part III Essay

Explain the role of representation in the "idea of America" and how it brought about the liberty that is the marvel of world history. Begin with natural law and include a discussion of the types of law that contribute to the American system of liberty with law.

"His will is our peace. It is that ocean vast whereunto are
moving all things which he creates and which nature makes."

Dante, *Paradiso*

Writing the Declaration of Independence

Nation Makers

Part IV:
The Impact of Christ on Religion, Education, and Government

CHRIST — Reform of Religion — Reform of Education — Reform of Government

How Christian Conscience, Character, and Reason Changed History

History tells a tragic story of man's inability to live by the natural law God built into the universe. From the Garden of Eden to the two tablets of law at Mount Sinai and beyond, the rebellion continued until God brought about his solution to the problem of sin by sending his Son and thus, writing the law on the heart of man through Christ. The focal point of all history has forever been the birth, death, and resurrection of the Son of God.

<u>At the coming of Christ, everything changed</u>. There was a new spirit when Christianity appeared. Man now could know that he was created in the divine image and destined for immortality. "This asserted for the individual an independent value . . . That man is superior to the state, which ought to be fashioned for his use. This was the advent of a new spirit and a new power in the world."[1]

The blessed sacrifice of the Lamb of God upon the Cross of Calvary offers the only true liberty to all who will accept Him as Redeemer and Savior. Men and women who yield themselves to Christ are self-governing individuals and need less and less the control of external law. This does not mean that they are "lawless," but rather, that as they fulfill the spirit of obedience to God, they fulfill the letter of obedience to the moral law and the laws of the land.

How did Christianity form the civil government that upholds the self-government and the individual freedom that became identified as distinctives of the American form of government?

Part IV answers that question and tells how Christ inspired the conscience, character, and reason of nine ordinary men to stand for truth and change history. These nine men from diverse backgrounds and places were used by God to give the American founders an understanding of the Gospel and thus the wisdom to apply truth to all of life, even civil government.

Part IV contains three major themes: The reform of religion, the reform of education, and the reform of law and government. These three major themes give substance to the "idea of America" and how the blessing of Christian self-government is the product of Christ His Story.

---

[1] Hall, *CHOC I*, 2.

Reform of Religion

The Reformers and the Bible in English

The period following the fall of the Roman Empire until the fourteenth century AD was a time when the light of truth flickered dimly throughout Europe and there was a famine of the Word of God as the Roman church preserved the Bible and worship in the Latin language.

It took nearly 1300 years for the church to work through the Scripture and form the doctrine to "Go therefore and make disciples of all the nations, baptizing them in the name of the Father and the Son and the Holy Spirit, teaching them to observe all that I commanded you…" As the church spread, so also human corruption used it as a means of subjecting the ignorant. Reform of the church was sorely needed.

The Reformers of religion each responded to the Word of God personally and then by taking a stand of conscience that often brought about their deaths. They knew that true reform required that the Bible be put in the hands of the people.

The Reformation was a movement that produced many reformers, but we will look closely at three: John Wycliffe in England, Martin Luther in Germany, and John Calvin in France.

At the end of this section of our study we will compare the contributions of each. Which one will you find most inspiring? As we discuss the Reformers, note the role the Bible played in their lives.

Wycliffe writing

John Wycliffe: "Morning Star of the Reformation" 1320–1384[2]

1. More than one hundred years before Luther, rose the *"morning-star of the Reformation"*, John Wycliffe, first in the line of evangelical reformers to whom the Gospel was the precious measure of reform. With Wycliffe's first beams in a dark age of anti-Christian idolatry occurred "the earliest break" with Latin Christianity. An important part of his ministry was to place the Bible in the heart of the individual. To do this, Wycliffe made one of the earliest translations of the Scriptures from the Latin into English.

2. "The principle that God's Word should be preached to the people, he expanded into the principle that Scripture must become the common property of all. As a means to this end, he saw the necessity of the Bible being translated into the language of the country, with the view of giving it the widest possible diffusion among the population ….

---

2 Slater, *T&L*, 166-168.

3. "To him the translation of the Bible was not an end in itself, but only a means to an end—that end being to place the Bible in the hands of his own countrymen, and to bring home the Word of God to the hearts of the English people. For this purpose copies of it were now made and circulated, not only of the whole Bible, but also of portions, and even of single books …."

4. "During the last years of Wycliffe's life his opponents evidently cherished the hope that his chief followers, already enfeebled and intimidated, would be hopelessly scattered after his death, and that the whole party would become extinct. Soon, however, it became plain that there was a life in the movement not at all dependent on the personality of Wycliffe. He was removed from the earthly scene; but his adherents continued his work with no appreciable diminution of energy. It was in the year succeeding the death of Wycliffe that the name of *Lollards* came into general use as a designation of his followers…. Its use by the hierarchy to characterize his followers is a proof to us that the 'Wycliffites' had become an independent sect, large enough to attract public attention, and formidable enough to arouse ecclesiastical animosity.

5. "The Lollard party, in the years immediately following Wycliffe's death, consisted, so to speak, of an inner and an outer circle. The former was composed of enthusiastic and able men, who in the first instance through the preaching of the Itinerants, and subsequently through their own reading and study, had been led to the adoption of evangelical principles. Thus it seemed to them all the more necessary, after the death of their venerated, strong-souled leader, to maintain the closest bonds of alliance for mutual encouragement and a common defense against their enemies.

6. "The outer and far larger circle comprised men and women, in different grades of society, who listened and read, learned and often believed. Many of these naturally passed into the inner circle, and became themselves the teachers of others. So numerous had the adherents of Wycliffe become during the period between his death and the close of the century that, according to the testimony of opponents, at least half the population had ranged themselves on the side of the Lollards. 'You could scarcely meet two persons in the road, but one of them would be a disciple of Wycliffe'"….

7. "They were, above all, characterized by a striving after holiness, a zeal for the spread of Scriptural truth, for the uprooting of prevalent error, and for Church reform. Even the common people among them were men who *believed*; and they communicated, as by a sacred contagion, their convictions to those around them. Thus they became mighty.

8. "Religious tracts had much to do with the dissemination of their doctrines… But above all the translation of the Bible became a power. It was largely circulated not only in a complete form, but in separate books; and wherever it was known an impulse was given to the Lollard doctrines…. The Bible being thus made a comparatively familiar book, great stress was laid upon the exposition of its contents by preaching. Staff in hand, the preachers journeyed on foot from place to place, and paused wherever they could obtain hearing from gentle or simple …

9. "The preaching, be it remembered, was in English; and the preachers were mainly of the same class as their hearers: their homely expositions of Scripture went home to the heart; they spoke, moreover, of prevailing sins and evils, as luxury and the like; they called by their right names the misdeeds of the clergy, while for themselves they sought nothing. It is no wonder that these travelling preachers stirred the land, and that the minds of men were attracted to them in a continually augmenting degree.

10. "Besides these open-air gatherings, assemblies were convened in halls and cottages, in chapels, in gardens. Here and there a little company would assemble to converse on Divine things, to build one another up in faith and knowledge. At such meetings the Bible in Wycliffe's translation would be read aloud, or a tract by Wycliffe or Hereford, explaining the sacred text. Even the art of reading would be taught on such occasions…. [It] was bitterly complain[ed] that the Word of God translated into English 'becomes more accessible and familiar to laymen and to women able to read than it had hithertofore been to the most intelligent and learned of the clergy …'

11. "The decree of the Council of Constance in regard to Wycliffe's bones was carried out after long delay … the remains of the great Englishman were not only torn from their resting-place, but burned to ashes and cast into the little river Swift, that runs by Lutterworth on its course to the Avon. Thus, in the often-quoted words of Thomas Fuller, **'the little river conveyed Wycliffe's remains into the Avon, the Avon into the Severn, Severn into the narrow seas, they to the main ocean. And thus the ashes of Wycliffe are the emblem of his doctrine, which now is dispersed all the world over'** [Prof. G.V. Lechler, D.D., *John Wycliffe and His English Precursors*]."

John Wycliffe died of a stroke in the parish church in 1384. He had been declared a heretic for speaking out against unbiblical teachings and practices in the church. It was for this reason that the church took vengeance forty-four years after his death at the Council of Constance. President Lincoln quoted Wycliffe in the Gettysburg Address when he said, "This Bible is for the government of the people, by the people and for the people."

What was Wycliffe's heart especially burdened to do and what did he do about it?

How did his followers demonstrate their adherence to the Gospel and how did they spread their work? What was the impact of the work of Wycliffe and his Lollards?

Does the art of reading have anything to do with the spread of Christianity?

How did men attempt to destroy the testimony of Wycliffe?

Why did Christians regard this event as evidence of God's work through Wycliffe?

Martin Luther—1482-1546[3]

"With Luther began the awakening of the human conscience. Terrified at the sin he discovered in himself, he found no other means of peace but faith in the grace of Christ Jesus. This starting-point of the German reformer was also that of every other Reformation."

Luther appealed to the authority of the Scriptures to challenge the divine right of papacy at the Diet of Worms in 1521.

" 'I am,' he pleaded, 'but a mere man, and not God; I shall therefore defend myself as Christ did, who said, 'If I have spoken evil, bear witness of the evil'.… For this reason, by the mercy of God I conjure you, most serene Emperor, and you, most illustrious electors and princes, and all men of every degree, to prove from the writings of the prophets and apostles that I have erred. As soon as I am convinced of this, I will retract every error, and will be the first to lay hold of my books, and throw them into the fire.… I cannot submit my faith either to the Pope or to the councils, because it is clear as the day that they have frequently erred and contradicted each other. Unless, therefore, I am convinced by the testimony of Scripture, or by clear reasoning, unless I am persuaded by means of the passages I have quoted, and unless my conscience is thus bound by the Word of God, I cannot and will not retract; for it is unsafe and injurious to act against one's own conscience. **Here I stand, I can do no other: may God help me! Amen.'**

"One of the sublimest scenes in history! No battle ever fought or won has been worth more to the cause of human liberty than this act of the peasant's son in asserting the claims of conscience before the dignitaries of Church and empire …

"By far the most important task, however, which occupied his leisure, was the translation of the Bible. The first draft of the New Testament was produced here. The work of the translation was continued at Wittenberg, until at length, in 1534, the complete Lutheran Bible was given to the people. The enterprise may well be regarded as marking an epoch in the national history. It is true that other translations into the vernacular had preceded this of Luther. But none of them had any thing like the same adaptation to the people; none of them were such homelike products to the German mind; none so brought out the riches of the German tongue; none were so true at once to the German and to the original; for, while it was a maxim with Luther that a translation must express the sense of the original, it was equally a maxim with him, that it must express that sense in the national idiom … 'A genuine son of his own people, gifted with all the wealth and depth of the German mind, he could enter into that age of simple national faith; he made its spirit and language his own,

---

3 Slater, *T&L*, 168-170.

and thus acquired the power of translating into German the religious-poetic and poetic-religious mode of expression.' It is scarcely necessary to add, that the copies of the new German Bible, issued as fast as the hard-worked presses could supply them, became powerful instruments for the spread of evangelical truth …

"Luther passed away (Feb. 18, 1546). His departure, as far as his personal fortunes were concerned, was in peace and unshaken faith. Among his last words was the thrice-repeated sentence: 'Father, into thy hands I commend my spirit. Thou hast redeemed me. Thou faithful God.' So ended a stormy life; so passed away one of the great men of history.… We see in him a marked individuality, an heroic temper, a consummate genius, a deeply religious spirit, a peculiarly faithful embodiment of strong national traits.

Luther Bible

"As David was the man of Israel, so Luther was the man of Germany. As David embodied the chivalry, the patriotism, the lyric talent, the domestic affection, and the religious ardor of Israel, so Luther embodied the leading features of the German heart and mind. His words thrilled the men of his time, and to-day are in large part fresh and living.… Heart and mind of the Germans were in his hand like the lyre in the hand of the musician. Moreover, he has given to his people more than any other man in Christian ages has ever given to a people, language, manual for popular instruction, Bible, hymns of worship . . . it is he only who has stamped the imperishable seal of his own soul alike upon the German language and upon the German mind [Henry C. Sheldon, *History of the Christian Church*]."

- What does Luther's cry, "Here I Stand, I can do no other: may God help me! Amen." mean for each individual Christian?

What was one of the greatest contributions that Luther made to the German people?

- Do you know what Luther did for Christian music? Write out the first verse of his most famous hymn.

Luther Songbook

A Mighty Fortress Is Our God

1. A mighty fortress is our God, a bulwark never failing;
Our helper he amid the flood of mortal ills prevailing.
For still our ancient foe doth seek to work us woe; his craft and power are great,
And armed with cruel hate, on earth is not his equal.

2. Did we in our own strength confide, our striving would be losing,
Were not the right man on our side, the man of God's own choosing.
Dost ask who that may be? Christ Jesus, it is he; Lord Sabaoth, his name,
From age to age the same, and he must win the battle.

3. And though this world, with devils filled, should threaten to undo us,
We will not fear, for God hath willed his truth to triumph through us.
The Prince of Darkness grim, we tremble not for him; his rage we can endure,
For lo, his doom is sure; one little word shall fell him.

4. That word above all earthly powers, no thanks to them, abideth;
The Spirit and the gifts are ours, thru him who with us sideth.
Let goods and kindred go, this mortal life also; the body they may kill;
God's truth abideth still; his kingdom is forever.

Composed in 1529, this is called the Battle Hymn of the Reformation. It was composed in 1529 when the German princes made formal "protest" against the revocation of their liberties and received the name "Protestants". This hymn has been translated into more languages than any other hymn.

John Calvin—1509-1564[4]

1. "The times of Luther were followed by those of Calvin. He, like his great predecessor, undertook to search the Scriptures, and in them found the same truth and the same life; but a different character distinguishes his work.

2. "The renovation of the individual, of the Church, and of the human race, is his theme. If the Holy Ghost kindles the lamp of truth in man, it is (according to Calvin) 'to the end that the entire man should be transformed.'—'In the kingdom of Christ,' he says, 'it is only the new man that flourishes and has any vigor, and whom we ought to take into account.'

3. "This renovation is, at the same time, an enfranchisement; and we might assign, as a motto to the reformation accomplished by Calvin, as well as to apostolical Christianity itself, these words of Jesus Christ: *The truth shall make you free.* John 8:32 …

4. "The reformation of the sixteenth century restored to the human race what the middle ages had stolen from them; it delivered them from the traditions, laws, and despotism of the papacy; it put an end to the minority and tutelage in which Rome claimed to keep mankind forever; and by calling upon man to establish his faith not on the words of a priest, but on the infallible Word of God, and by announcing to every one free access to the Father through the new and saving way—Christ Jesus, it proclaimed and brought about the hour of Christian manhood…

5. "There are, no doubt, many countries, especially among those which the sun of Christianity has not yet illumined, that are without civil liberty, and that groan under the arbitrary rule of powerful masters. But, in order to become free outwardly, men must first succeed in being free inwardly …

6. "The liberty which the Truth brings is not for individuals only: it affects the whole of society. Calvin's work of renovation, in particular, which was doubtless first of all an internal work, was afterwards destined to exercise a great influence over nations.

7. "In intellect, Calvin was undoubtedly one of the most remarkable men of the sixteenth century. The mere amount of work that he accomplished in the space of about thirty years attests extraordinary capacity. His routine duties as a teacher, preacher, and administrator, were such that it is difficult to conceive how there

---

4 Slater, *T&L*, 170-172.

could have been time or strength for other tasks.... He carried on an extensive correspondence, responding with much pains-taking to the manifold inquiries which came from the great multitude that owned him as the master mind among all the leaders in the religious revolution. He assisted in preparing the translation of the Bible which passed into general use among the French Protestants... His commentaries, distinguished for lucidity, terseness, and rational attention to the trend of each writing, covered the larger part of the Bible... Crowning all, was his great work in systematic theology, to which he gave the finishing touch five years before his death.

8. "The scale on which Geneva exercised the function of a training-school may be estimated from the fact that at one time, according to the report of a contemporary, Calvin had regularly a thousand hearers for his theological lectures; and also by the fact that the Academy of Geneva, which was opened in 1559, enrolled during its first year nine hundred students...."

9. "The reasons for the wide and penetrating influence of Calvin have been indicated in the account of his character and work. He organized an intellectual system for the reform movement, and gave incisive expression to the ideas that were struggling in the minds of his contemporaries. The masculine tone to his writings took a strong hold upon a great multitude of men, and infused into them something of his own energy and resoluteness of spirit. Having the temper of the lawgiver, as well as that of the logician, he gave an unique stress to the ethical demands of Christianity, and urged powerfully <u>the need of realizing the truth of God in practice, as well as acknowledging it in theory</u>. Not a little of that stern practical energy, that readiness to carry out convictions, which has been manifested in various sections of the Reformed Church, was born of Calvin's spirit and teaching …

10. "The immense labors of Calvin involved premature exhaustion of body.... He passed away in peace on the 27th of May, 1564. "… the characteristic element of the Genevese Reform is liberty.... The necessity of liberty for the Gospel and of the Gospel for liberty is now acknowledged by all thoughtful men; but it was proclaimed by the history of Geneva three centuries ago.… It is in this small republic that we find men remarkable for their devotion to liberty, for their attachment to law, for the boldness of their thoughts, the firmness of their character, and the strength of their energy....''

11. "Lastly, Calvin was the founder of the greatest of republics. The 'pilgrims' who left their country in the reign of James I and, landing on the barren shores of New England, founded populous and mighty colonies, are his sons, his direct and legitimate sons; and <u>that American nation which we have seen growing so rapidly boasts as its father</u> the humble reformer on the shores of the Leman. [J. H. Merle D'Aubigne, *History of the Reformation in Europe*]"

What is the suggested "motto" for the reformation accomplished by Calvin? What principle of liberty taught by John Calvin had to be the basis of political liberty?

Explain "in order to become free outwardly, men must first succeed in being free inwardly".

Summarize the work and accomplishments of John Calvin.

Discuss the similarities and differences in the work and contribution of Wycliffe, Luther, and Calvin.

The Story of the Bible in English[5]

"It is difficult today to realize that there was ever a time when the bible—our holy scriptures—was not available to everyone. That is why this is one of the greatest stories ever told in Christian History. So precious were the words and the teachings of Christ Jesus that although they were spoken in a decaying language the providence of God brought them forth:

"The story of how our Scriptures were translated into English is one all Christians should know. For only Christian love could have brought forth the Word and made it available to the individual. Despite persecution, imprisonment and martyrdom the efforts of those devoted men of God did indeed bring to us today the Book of books. The story tells of the man whose life work with the Scriptures contributed so much to making the word available to each one of us."

The Reformers all purposed to translate the Bible into the "vernacular" – the language of the people. Translating the Bible is a monumental task requiring the knowledge of ancient languages and much study. However, our courageous and spirited Reformers realized the need of man for the revealed law–the Word of God.

William Tyndale Printing His Translation Of The Bible Into English At Cologne A.D. 1525

The Wycliffe Bible—1380[6]

"Wycliffe's Teutonic love of truth, of freedom and of independence … moved him to give his countrymen the open Scripture as their best safeguard and protection … and it was the development of the English language into a literary medium of expression … which first made a people's Bible possible … And if Wycliffe represents a new movement in our literature, so too does he represent a new departure in our religious history. For the rise of Lollardy, in so far as it was a religious movement, marks the earliest break in the … continuity of Latin Christianity in England."

The Tyndale Bible—1526

"Tyndale is the true father of our present English Bible.… It has been estimated that, of Tyndale's work as above specified, our Bibles retain at the present day something like eighty per cent, in the Old Testament, and ninety per cent, in the New. If this estimate may be accepted no grander tribute could be paid to the industry, scholarship, and genius of the pioneer whose indomitable resolution enabled him to persevere in labours prolonged through twelve long years of exile from the land that in his own words he so 'loved and longed for' with the practical certainty of a violent death staring him all the while in the face."

---

5 Slater, *T&L*, 333-334.
6 Slater, *T&L*, 332-333.

THE GREAT BIBLE—1539

"Within twelve months of the martyrdom of its author at Vilvorde, (Tyndale) the translation which 'either with glosses (marginal notes) or without' had been denounced, abused, and burnt at St. Paul's, was now, under its assumed name (the Matthew Bible) formerly approved by the King's grace, and published, together with Coverdale's Bible, under the shelter of a royal proclamation and license … In April 1539, the first edition of this magnificent specimen of the art of printing was ready for publication."

THE GENEVA BIBLE—1559

"In many ways this edition formed a new departure and offered new attractions. Especially was this the case with regard to bulk.… In the place of the heavy black letters to which the readers had been accustomed, there appeared the clear Roman type with which our modern press has made us familiar. The division of the chapters into verses … has undeniable advantages."

THE KING JAMES BIBLE—1611

"In 1611 the Authorized Version, a folio volume in black-letter type, was issued to the public. It had no notes, and the interpretation of it was therefore left perfectly free.… The predominance of Saxon words in this version is very remarkable. As compared with Latin words they actually constitute some nine-tenths of it … In the Lord's Prayer no less than fifty-nine words out of sixty-five are of Saxon origin … They had ready to hand the rich results of nearly a century of diligent and unintermittent labour in the field of Biblical study. The great lines which were to be followed had long since been marked out by Wycliffe, Tyndale, and Coverdale, while useful side-lights could be derived from the Latin and modern translations above enumerated."

This version of the Bible has particular significance for the course of Christian History and the advancement of Christianity. We note the predominance of Saxon words as compared with Latin words, and, again, in the fullness of God's time, the English language had reached that peak of its richness—its full flowering. So did God's Word crown this period of the blossoming of English literature.

Most important, however, was the fact that this was the *freest* and *purest* of Bible translations since Wycliffe's first work. This edition had no notes and "the interpretation of it was therefore left perfectly free." This was a Bible relying wholly on the power of the Word to reveal its holy message!

 What was important about the King James Bible for all Christians?

Which Bible helped to initiate evangelism in England? Which Bible was the contribution of a martyr? Which Bible is known in the printing world as a magnificent specimen of the art of printing? Which Bible was the first Bible to divide the Scriptures into chapters?

The Martyrdom of William Tyndale[7]

"Although it was against the law to distribute translations of the Bible in English, one particular man took on the task, had to flee the country, and was ultimately burned at the stake as a heretic. Many more were martyred for having and preaching the Bible in English. William Tyndale produced a full translation of the Bible in defiance of the King, exiling himself in Europe until it was done.

---
7 Slater, *T&L*, 334-337.

"*Foxe's Book of Martyrs* tells us Tyndale said, "I defy the Pope, and all his laws; and if God spares my life, ere many years, I will cause the boy that driveth the plow to know more of the Scriptures than the Pope!"[8] Within four years of his martyrdom, four English translations of the Bible were published in England at the King's behest, including Henry's official Great Bible. All were based on Tyndale's work.

"The Holy Scriptures, translated, studied, circulated, and preached since the fourteenth century by Wycliffe and his disciples, became in the sixteenth century, by the publication of Erasmus' Testament, and the translations of Tyndale and Coverdale, the powerful instrument of a real evangelical revival, and created the scriptural reformation …

"Most of the reformers, Luther, Zwingli, Calvin, Knox, and others have acquired that name by their preachings, their writings, their struggles, and their actions. It is not so with the principal reformer of England: all his activity was concentrated in the Holy Scriptures…. One man, desirous of reviving the Church of Christ in England, had made the translation of the Holy Scriptures the work of his life. Tyndale had been forced to leave his country; but he had left it only to prepare seed which, borne on the wings of the wind, was to change the wildernesses of Great Britain into a fruitful garden.

"Tyndale … was in prison at Vilvorde, near Brussels. In vain was he girt around with the thick walls of that huge fortress. Tyndale was free. 'There is the captivity and bondage,' he could say, 'whence Christ delivered us, redeemed and loosed us. His blood, his death, his patience in suffering rebukes and wrongs, his prayers and fastings, his meekness and fulfilling of the uttermost point of the law broke the bonds of Satan, wherein we were so strait bound.' Thus Tyndale was as truly free at Vilvorde, as Paul had been at Rome. He felt pressed to accomplish <u>a vow made many years before. 'If God preserves my life', he had said, 'I will cause a boy that driveth a plow to know more of the Scriptures than the pope.'</u> True Christianity shows itself by the attention it gives to Christ's little ones. It was time for Tyndale to keep his promise. He occupied his prison hours in preparing for the humble dwellers in the Gloucestershire villages and the surrounding counties, an edition of the Bible in which he employed the language and orthography used in that part of England …

> **How beautiful on the mountains are the feet of him that brings good tidings, that publishes peace; that brings good tidings of good, that publishes salvation; that said to Zion, Your God reigns!**
>
> Isaiah 52:7

"The Holy Scriptures have been written in English with the blood of martyrs—if we may so speak—the blood of Fryth, Tyndale, and Rogers: it is a crown of glory for that translation. At the moment of Tyndale's perfidious arrest, Rogers had fortunately saved the manuscript of the Old Testament, and now resolved to delay the printing no longer. When the news of this reached the Reformer in his cell at Vilvorde, it cast a gleam of light upon his latter days and filled his heart with joy. The *whole* Bible,—that was the legacy which the dying Tyndale desired to leave to his fellow-countrymen. He took pleasure in his gloomy dungeon in following with his mind's eye that divine Scripture from city to city and from cottage to cottage; his imagination pictured to him the struggles it would have to go through, and also its victories … [J.H. Merle D'Aubigne, *History of the Reformation in Europe*]."

"This man, so active, so learned, and so truly great, whose works circulated far and wide with so much power, had at the same time within him a pure and beneficent light—the love of God and of man—which shed its mild rays on all around him. The depth of his faith, the charm of his conversation, the uprightness of his conduct, touched those who came near him. The jailer liked to bring him his food, in order to talk

---

8 John Foxe, *Foxe's Book of Martyrs*, (Fleming H. Revell, 1998), 139.

with him, and his young daughter often accompanied him and listened eagerly to the words of the pious Englishman. Tyndale spoke of Jesus Christ; it seemed to him that the riches of the divine Spirit were about to transform Christendom.… The jailer, his daughter, and other members of their house were converted to the Gospel by Tyndale's life and doctrine.

"However dark the machinations of his enemies, they could not obscure the divine light kindled in his heart, and which shone before men. There was an invincible power in this Christian man. Full of hope in the final victory of Jesus Christ, he courageously trampled under foot tribulations, trials, and death itself. He believed in the victory of the Word. 'I am bound like a malefactor,' he said, 'but the Word of God is not bound.' The bitterness of his last days was changed into great peace and divine sweetness …

"Friday, the 6th of October, 1536 was the day that terminated the miserable but glorious life of the reformer.… On arriving at the scene of punishment, the reformer found a numerous crowd assembled. The government had wished to show the people the punishment of a heretic, but they only witnessed the triumph of a martyr. Tyndale was calm. 'I call God to record,' he could say, 'that I have never altered, against the voice of my conscience, one syllable of his Word. Nor would do this day, if all the pleasures, honors, and riches of the earth might be given me.' The joy of hope filled his heart: yet one painful idea took possession of him. Dying far from his country, abandoned by his king, he felt saddened at the thought of that prince, who had already persecuted so many of God's servants, and who remained obstinately rebellious against that divine light which everywhere shone around him. Tyndale would not have that soul perish through carelessness. His charity buried all the faults of the monarch: he prayed that those sins might be blotted out from before the face of God; he would have saved Henry VIII at any cost.

"While the executioner was fastening him to the post the reformer exclaimed in a loud and suppliant voice: 'Lord, open the king of England's eyes!' They were his last words. Instantly afterwards he was strangled, and flames consumed the martyr's body. His last cry was wafted to the British Isles, and repeated in every assembly of Christians. A great death crowned a great life. 'Such,' says the old chronicler, John Foxe, 'such is the story of that true servant and martyr of God, William Tyndale, who, for his notable pains and travail, may well be called *the Apostle of England in this our later Age.*'

"His fellow-countrymen profited by the work of his life. As early as 1526 more than twenty editions of Tyndale's New Testament had been circulated over the kingdom, and others had followed them. It was like a mighty river continually bearing new waters to the sea. Did the reformer's death dry them up suddenly? No. A greater work still was to be accomplished: the entire Bible was ready. But could it be circulated? The king had refused his consent to the circulation of Coverdale's Bible; would he not do the same with this, and with greater reason?…

"Henry ran over the book: Tyndale's name was not in it, and the dedication to his Majesty was very well written. The King regarding (and not without reason) Holy Scripture as the most powerful engine to destroy the papal system, and believing that this translation would help him to emancipate England from the Romish domination, came to an unexpected resolution: he authorized the sale and the reading of the Bible throughout the kingdom ….

William Tyndale imprisoned

"Whoever possessed the means bought the book and read it or had it read to him by others. Aged persons learnt their letters in order to study the Holy Scriptures of God. In many places there were meetings for reading; poor people clubbed their savings together and purchased a Bible, and then in some remote corner of the church they modestly formed a circle, and read the Holy Book between them …

"In all the towns and villages of Tyndale's country the holy pages were opened, and the delighted readers found therein those treasures of peace and joy which the martyr had known. Many cried out with him, 'We know that this Word is from God, as we know that fire burns; not because any one has told us, but because a Divine fire consumes our hearts. O the brightness of the face of Moses! O the splendor of the glory of Jesus Christ, which no veil conceals! O the inward power of the Divine word, which compels us with so much sweetness, to love and to do! O the temple of God within us, in which the Son of God dwells!' Tyndale had desired to see the world on fire by his Master's Word, and that fire was kindled."

What was the vow Tyndale made? How could he declare himself free yet in prison?

List the qualities of character observed in Tyndale.

What is the most extraordinary thing about the martyrdom of Tyndale?

What was the impact of the Tyndale Bible in England?

Do you recognize similarities among the Reformers in their character, conscience, and the results of their lives and work? Discuss.

William Tyndale strangled and burned

Part IV: The Impact of Christ on Religion, Education, and Government

Peter Ramus

Reform of Education

About the time Tyndale was translating the Bible into English in Antwerp, and Henry VIII was burning heretics at the stake in London, and only a few years after Columbus sailed to America, Pierre de la Ramée was born in Paris in 1515.

As a young scholar at the University of Paris, Pierre de la Ramée or, in English, Peter Ramus, was steeped in the medieval form of education called scholasticism. Scholasticism was based on Greek philosophy that kept man in a state of subjection to the material powers that be. Its philosophy, based on Aristotle's writings, omitted God, advocated a secular approach to all knowledge, and favored disputation—argument—as the method of learning.

Peter Ramus loved learning but found that his scholastic education left him "not more learned . . . nor more skilled . . . nor wiser in anything" after years of labor.[9]

Although he dedicated his life to the Medieval church, on August 26, 1572 during the St. Bartholomew's Day Massacre, Ramus was martyred. Five thousand Huguenots (French Protestants) were murdered in the streets. Ramus' martyrdom was with extreme hatred and excessive brutality. He was found at home, thrown from his chamber window, dragged through streets, beaten by his tutors, dismembered by the 'churchmen,' beheaded, and his remains thrown into the river Seine.

How can we understand the source of such savage hatred?

His honesty and desire for real education set off an explosion that still echoes today. In 1536 at the age of 21, bold Peter Ramus dared to stand for his Masters degree before his teachers and colleagues and declare: "All that Aristotle said is false!"[10] "This announcement was the first blast in the educational reformation of the 16th and 17th centuries. Without it the theological Reformation begun by Luther and Calvin might not ever have been sustained."[11] Ramus' problem was he thought like a Protestant! He was inspired by the Protestant Reformation and natural law to bring education to a Biblical base.

---

9 Frank Pierrepont Graves, *Peter Ramus and the Educational Reformation of the Sixteenth Century,* (MacMillan Co., 1912), 23.
10 Graves, *Peter Ramus and the Educational Reformation of the Sixteenth Century*, 26.
11 Rebecca H. Beach, "*Abstract and Four Articles: Technometrics of PA, Recovering William Ames, Recovering Peter Ramus, Confront the War on Language — Noah Webster's 1828,*" 2014, MS, Sacramento.

Peter Ramus abandoned the ineffective, Greek methods of the university and began to teach according to what he understood to be truth, and students found his teaching clear, thoughtful, productive, and useful and flocked to him and his classes. He pioneered a new kind of education by defining the arts (subjects) in simple textbooks that went into universities and classrooms. His new "Method" of education, "mastered at the age of about twelve, it was not to be taken up again at any higher level, though of course, it was to be practiced all the time and everywhere. Once you 'had' it, you had it cold." [12]

His booklets spread across Europe. His ideas revolutionized teaching in the universities of Europe and England. He continued his writing and publishing until he had addressed all subjects with his Method and set in place the reformation of Education. His "method" became the tool of learning that reached into the 16th, 17th, and 18th centuries in England, Holland, Germany, and America. An examination of Harvard graduation theses show the Ramean method widely used in our Colonial universities and by our Colonial clergy to educate generations of Americans who would reach a level of education rarely equaled in the world.

In fact, Ramean reforms were the impetus in our founding era to bring a unity of thought and principle based upon natural and revealed law that eventually formed the United States of America.

This unity of thought and principle owes its substance to a student of Peter Ramus, William Ames. Ames learned the Ramean method in England as a student at Cambridge where he was taught by Puritans. Ames used the Ramean method to write a comprehensive theology – *The Marrow of Sacred Divinity* – a book that became the textbook of theology in America studied by generations of students.

In colonial American education, theology was taught as a centerpiece of the curriculum. The Ames theology arrived at the early Plimoth Plantation and remained central in the education of the era. *The Marrow of Divinity* identifies faith and practice as it related to all of life including government. Our Founders understood principles of Christian government, particularly the principles of self-government from the teaching of William Ames.

Ramean reforms is the "precursor of the Principle Approach,®" [13] practiced at Harvard, Yale, Princeton and used by Colonial clergy in preaching and educating the generations who learned to reason Biblically so that they could, by reason and revelation, achieve the first civil liberty of conscience in history, fulfilling His Story.

The intellectual reformation inspired by Ramus' work set the stage for "America's golden age: an age when . . .

America's goodness made her great —

> An age when America's Biblical reasoning undergirded her homes and churches.

> An age when America's civil government elevated the individual above the state, declared the equality of all men, and honored man's God given rights. [14]

> It explains America's exceptionalism among nations.

Discuss: Explain the remarkable role of Peter Ramus in the Reformation of education.

Write: What caused Ramus to speak up and change direction in his method of teaching?

Write: How did Peter Ramus directly impact the development of liberty in America?

---

12 Walter J. Ong, "Homiletic," Journal of the History of Ideas, 14 (1953), 235-248.
13 James B. Rose, "Peter Ramus and William Ames: French and English Precursors to the Principle Approach," *The Journal of the Foundation for American Christian Education* VI (1994-1995): 13-21.
14 Rebecca H. Beach and Carole G. Adams, *"Finding the Real Common Core of American Christian Education: The Theology of American Liberty"* (speech, Reason for Hope, Virginia, Virginia, Beach, February 11, 2015).

Reform of Law and Government

The Gospel is the good news of God's mercy and grace that offers each of us eternal life. But the power of the Gospel impacts every area of life including particularly how men are governed. After the reformation of the church and the availability of the Bible in English, men began applying the Gospel to every practical area of life, just as God intended. It wasn't long before it became clear that the liberty Jesus proclaimed should be translated into the civil sphere — how men are governed. This thinking was particularly influential in England in limiting the power of the monarchy and calling forth increasing degrees of self-government.

The Britons inherited a love of liberty from their Anglo-Saxon forbearers. This tendency is seen in their earliest document of liberty, the Magna Charta, and increases as the Gospel is proclaimed and the understanding of self-government becomes known after the Reformation.

We will look at the documents that carry the ideas that came to fruition in America.

King John of England, 1167-1216. Illuminated manuscript

English Constitutional Law: Liberty Under Law

The tendency of the true Gospel principles is to bring the most absolute despotism under the limits of the law; to imbue limited monarchies more and more with the spirit of popular institutions; to prepare the people to govern themselves; and finally to establish everywhere the spirit and the reality, if not the very forms of a republic.[15]

One of the efforts leading to the establishment of American Constitutional government has been for Christianity to define in the civil sphere the rights and privileges of each individual. As we learned, Rome decreed the privileges of citizenship by her laws or edicts. She proclaimed the special rights of Roman citizenship to exist by virtue of the power of Rome. When the Roman Empire fell, so did the rights of citizenship. This is government from the "top down" granting rights to the individual.

In England where Christianity had been influencing custom and usage for several centuries, it is not surprising that by the thirteenth century the first efforts to identify greater individual freedom would be in evidence.

In 1215 the English barons who demanded from King John a written charter of liberties, which we know today as Magna Charta or The Great Charter, laid the first stepping-stone to the American Bill of Rights. The Charter did not establish any new constitutional principles but it began to make their meaning more precise and it began to spell out what the rights of the individual really meant.

---

15 Edwin Hall, *The Puritans and their Principles*, (Baker & Scribner, 1846), 300.

Magna Charta—1215[16]

America's Christian establishment as a nation enabled her to do something which no other nation had ever been able to do—namely to identify the Rights of man as God-given and God-granted. This enabled America to set forth these rights and to establish Christianity's form of government—Christian Self-Government—which is government predicated upon liberty under law and which represents the rights and liberties of each individual under the law. This is the culmination of the Christian idea of man and government.

England did much to establish the rights of the individual as law. But these rights had to be *granted* by the monarchy to its citizens. America established a Christian precedent by being the first nation to define the rights of the individual as *God-granted* and thus as the sacred *property* of the individual—the *preservation and protection* of this property was deemed as the *chief end of government*.

As we read the Magna Charta today with its many strange sounding terms, we can begin to see the thread of individual liberty running through. In order to appreciate what a victory the Magna Charta was we need to glimpse Feudal England at the time of King John.

Magna Charta signed by King John at Runneymeade 1215

"Magna Charta was the culmination of a protest against the arbitrary rule of King John, who was using governmental powers which had been established by the great builders of the English nation, William the Conqueror, Henry I, and Henry II, for selfish and tyrannical purposes. In general, these abuses took the pattern of increasing customary feudal obligations and decreasing established feudal rights and privileges. The barons were forced to pay taxes above the usual rate, and their right to hold court for their tenants was restricted. The king exerted pressure in order to influence church elections. The merchants of London were burdened by heavy taxes, and their trading privileges were curtailed. To a limited extent even the lowest of King John's subjects suffered because his confiscation of church property destroyed the only available source of poor relief …"The final crisis of the reign began … when John sought to revive the war with the king of France. The barons refused to follow their king to battle, and John prepared to march against them to compel obedience. The barons rallied around Stephen Langton, who produced in their midst a copy of Henry I's Charter of Liberties. The barons then resolved to fight for those liberties 'even unto death'… John's last hope of success disappeared when the merchants of London turned against him and opened the gates to the insurgents. With only a small band of supporters remaining, John at last agreed to meet the demands of the barons. The dramatic meeting occurred on June 15, 1215 at Runnymede, along the banks of the Thames… The articles presented by the barons were agreed to and sealed, and during the next few days copies of Magna Charta were drawn up in final form and sealed by the King [*Sources of Our Liberties,* edited by Richard L. Perry, 1959, American Bar Foundation, Chicago, Illinois]."

---

16 Slater, *T&L*, 344-346.

John Locke reminds us that under the "Law of Nature … i.e. the Will of God" "no one ought to harm another in his Life, Health, Liberty, or Possessions". Why this consideration of each other?

Now after centuries of permitting only certain individuals in a society to have protection of *body* and *property*, the Magna Charta sets forth certain rights which are to belong to every *"freeman"*. This doesn't cover everyone who lives in the kingdom yet, but it is a big step forward.

The most important clauses of the Magna Charta can be traced down through our own Bill of Rights. What do these terms mean to you?

   a) the protection of the *writ of habeas corpus*

   b) the rights of *trial by jury*

   c) the guarantee that no person can be deprived of life, liberty or property without *due process of law*

Discuss the significance of the Magna Charta to the American Bill of Rights.

List the purpose and the key points of the Magna Charta.

Petition of Right – 1628

Today in America many groups are taking their grievances directly in person to the streets in rioting, or demanding the courts make decisions in areas beyond their intended jurisdiction. This is not a Christian or Constitutional approach. There are means by which a people governed by a Constitution could take steps to correct what they consider as unjust encroachments or infringements of their rights.

Discuss the following definitions in preparation to discuss English Constitutional law:

> GRIE´VANCE, n. [from grief.] *That which causes grief or uneasiness; that which burdens, oppresses or injures, implying a sense of wrong done, or a continued injury, and therefore applied only to the effects of human conduct; never to providential evils. The oppressed subject has the right to petition for a redress of grievances.*
>
> EN CRŌACH, v. i. *Primarily, to catch as with a hook. Hence, To enter on the rights and possessions of another; to intrude; to take possession of what belongs to another, by gradual advances into his limits or jurisdiction, and usurping a part of his rights or prerogatives; with on. The farmer who runs a fence on his neighbor's land, and incloses a piece with his own encroaches on his neighbor's property. It is important to prevent one branch of government from encroaching on the jurisdiction of another.*
>
> PETI´´TION, n. 2. *A formal request or supplication, verbal or written; particularly, a written supplication from an inferior to a superior, either to a single person clothed with power, or to a legislative or other body, soliciting some favor, grant, right or mercy.*

Petitioning the king and parliament as a Christian and later Constitutional means of redressing wrongs done in the civil sphere became a pattern of action for the American colonists.

The most notable example in history of a people patiently petitioning their monarch for redress of rights is during the years before the American Revolution—or the War of Independence of the American people for their separation from Great Britain. Our Declaration of Independence demonstrates honorable and respectful petition. The English Petition of Right in 1628 is forerunner to our Declaration.

The Petition of Right[17]

On the 5th day of June, 1628, the House of Commons presented the most extraordinary spectacle, perhaps in all its history. The famous Petition of Right had been passed by both Houses, and the royal answer had just been received. Its tone was that of gracious assent, but it omitted the necessary legal formalities, and the Commons well knew what this meant. They were to be tricked with sweet words, and the petition was not to acquire the force of a statute.

How was it possible to deal with such a slippery creature? There was but one way of saving the dignity of the throne without sacrificing the liberty of the people, and that was to hold the king's ministers responsible to Parliament, in anticipation of modern methods. It was accordingly proposed to impeach the Duke of Buckingham before the House of Lords.

The Speaker now "brought an imperious message from the king, … warning them that he would not tolerate any aspersion upon his ministers." Nothing daunted by this, Sir John Eliot arose to lead the debate, when the Speaker called him to order in view of the king's message. "Amid a deadly stillness" Eliot sat down and burst into tears. For a moment the House was overcome with despair. Deprived of all constitutional methods of redress, they suddenly saw yawning before them the direful alternative—slavery or civil war. Since the day of Bosworth a hundred and fifty years had passed without fighting worthy of mention on English soil, such an era of peace as had hardly ever before been seen on the earth; now half the Nation was to be pitted against the other half, families were to be divided against themselves, as in the dreadful days of the Roses, and with what consequences no one could foresee.

"Let us sit in silence," quoth Sir Dudley Digges, "we are miserable, we know not what to do!" Nay, cried Sir Nathaniel Rich, "we must now speak, or forever hold our peace." Then did grim Mr. Prynne and Sir Edward Coke mingle their words with sobs, while there were few dry eyes in the House. Presently they found their voices, and used them in a way that rung from the startled king his formal assent to the Petition of Right [John Fiske, *The Beginnings of New England, or the Puritan Theocracy in its Relations to Civil and Religious Liberty*, Boston, MA: Houghton, Mifflin and Company, 1898, 104–106]."

The Petition of Right was another stepping stone spelling out in even greater detail specific rights of Englishmen. We can think of it as constitutional law identifying for the individual the areas where a monarch cannot encroach. This was particularly needed in England where the kings had for centuries ruled as absolute monarchs without asking permission from any man, because they believed they were kings by divine authority. The Petition of Right of 1628 considered one of the three crucial constitutional documents of England, along with the Magna Charta and the Bill of Rights 1689.

Examine and Discuss the Petition of Right, noticing its spirit of petition.

---

17 Hall, *CHOC* I, 41-42.

The Petition of Right[18]

Humbly show unto our Sovereign Lord the King, the Lords, Spiritual and Temporal, and Commons in Parliament assembled, that whereas it is declared and enacted by a statute made in the time of the reign of King Edward the First, commonly called Statutum de tallagio non concedendo, that no tallage or aid shall be laid or levied by the King or his heirs in this realm, without the good will and assent of the Archbishops, Bishops, Earls, Barons, Knights, Burgesses, and other the freemen of the commonalty of this realm: and by authority of Parliament holden in the five and twentieth year of the reign of King Edward the Third, it is declared and enacted, that from thenceforth no person shall be compelled to make any loans to the King against his will, because such loans were against reason and the franchise of the land; and by other laws of this realm it is provided, that none should be charged by any charge or imposition, called a Benevolence, nor by such like charge: by which, the statutes before-mentioned, and other the good laws and statutes of this realm, your subjects have inherited this freedom, that they should not be compelled to contribute to any tax, tallage, aid, or other like charge, not set by common consent in Parliament: …

III. And where also by the statute called, 'The Great Charter of the Liberties of England,' it is declared and enacted, that no freeman may be taken or imprisoned or be disseised of his freehold or liberties, or his free customs, or be outlawed or exiled, or in any manner destroyed, but by the lawful judgment of his peers, or by the law of the land:

IV. And in the eight and twentieth year of the reign of King Edward the Third, it was declared and enacted by authority of Parliament, that no man of what estate or condition that he be, should be put out of his lands or tenements, nor taken, nor imprisoned, nor disherited, nor put to death, without being brought to answer by due process of law: …

VI. And whereas of late great companies of soldiers and mariners have been dispersed into divers counties of the realm, and the inhabitants against their wills have been compelled to receive them into their houses, and there to suffer them to sojourn, against the laws and customs of this realm, and to the great grievance and vexation of the people.

VII. And whereas also by authority of Parliament, in the 25th year of the reign of King Edward the Third, it is declared and enacted, that no man shall be forejudged of life or limb against the form of the Great Charter, and the law of the land; and by the said Great Charter and other the laws and statutes of this your realm, no man ought to be adjudged to death, but by the laws established in this your realm, either by the customs of the same realm or by Acts of Parliament: …

X. They do therefore humbly pray your Most Excellent Majesty, that no man hereafter be compelled to make or yield any gift, loan, benevolence, tax, or such like charge, without common consent by Act of Parliament; and that none be called to make answer, or take such oath, or to give attendance, or be confined, or otherwise molested or disquieted concerning the same, or for refusal thereof; and that no freeman, in any such manner as is before-mentioned, be imprisoned or detained; and that your Majesty will be pleased to remove the said soldiers and mariners, and that your people may not be so burdened in time to come; and that the aforesaid commissions for proceeding by martial law, may be revoked and annulled; and that hereafter no commissions of like nature may issue forth to any person or persons whatsoever, to be executed as aforesaid, lest by colour of them any of your Majesty's subjects be destroyed or put to death, contrary to the laws and franchise of the land.

XI. All which they most humbly pray of your Most Excellent Majesty, as their rights and liberties according to the laws and statutes of this realm: and that your Majesty would also vouchsafe declare, that the awards, doings, and proceedings to the prejudice of your people, in any of the premises, shall not be drawn hereafter into consequence or example: and that your Majesty would be also graciously pleased, for the further comfort and safety of your people, to declare your royal will and pleasure, that in the things aforesaid all your officers and ministers shall serve you, according to the laws and statutes of this realm, as they tender the honour of your Majesty, and the prosperity of this kingdom.

---

18 George Burton Adams and H. Morse Stephens, eds., *Select Documents of English Constitutional History* (MacMillan Company, 1901), 339-342.

Rights and Liberties

As the Word of God became more solidly infused into the thinking of the Reformers, philosophers of government, and the people, the love of liberty and its principles emerged and took power over the centralized and often tyrannical structure of government in England. From the *Magna Charta*, through the Reformation, and finally to the Petition of Right, came the English Bill of Rights.

The Bill of Rights is an act of the Parliament of England that deals with constitutional matters and sets out certain basic civil rights. It was passed on 16 December 1689, presented to William and Mary in February 1689, inviting them to become joint sovereigns of England. The Bill of Rights lays down limits on the powers of the monarch and sets out the rights of Parliament, including the requirement for regular parliaments, free elections, and freedom of speech in Parliament. It sets out certain rights of individuals including the prohibition of cruel and unusual punishment and reestablishes the liberty of Protestants to have arms for their defense within the rule of law.

The **English Bill of Rights** was another stepping stone further limiting the power of the king over the individual citizen. It was the direct ancestor to our American Bill of Rights—the first ten amendments to the United States Constitution.

English Bill Of Rights[19]
Westminster, December 16, 1689

WHEREAS the lords spiritual and temporal and commons assembled at Westminster lawfully, fully and freely representing all the estates of the people of this realm, did upon the thirteenth day of February in the year of our Lord one thousand six hundred eighty-eight, present unto Their Majesties, then called and known by the names and style of William and Mary, prince and princess of Orange, being present in their proper persons, a Certain declaration in writing made by the said lords and commons in the words following viz.:

Whereas the late king James the Second by the assistance of divers evil counsellors, judges and ministers employed by him did endeavour to subvert and extirpate the Protestant religion and the laws and liberties of this kingdom.

By assuming and exercising a power of dispensing with and suspending of laws, and the execution of laws, without consent of parliament.

By committing and prosecuting divers worthy prelates for humbly petitioning to be excused from concurring to the said assumed power.

By issuing and causing to be executed a commission under the great seal for erecting a court, called the court of commissioners for ecclesiastical causes.

By levying money for and to the use of the crown, by pretence of prerogative, for other time and in other manner than the same was granted by parliament.

By raising and keeping a standing army within this kingdom in time of peace, without consent of parliament, and quartering of soldiers contrary to law.

By causing several good subjects being Protestants to be disarmed, at the same time when papists were both armed and employed, contrary to law.

By violating the freedom of election of members to serve in parliament.

By prosecutions in the court of king's bench for matters and causes cognizable only in parliament, and by divers other arbitrary and illegal courses.

And whereas of late years partial, corrupt and unqualified persons have been returned and served on juries in trials, and particularly divers jurors in trials for high treason, which were not freeholders.

And excessive bail hath been required of persons committed in criminal cases, to elude the benefit of the laws made for the liberty of the subjects.

And excessive fines have been imposed.

And illegal and cruel punishments have been inflicted.

And several grants and promises made of fines and forfeitures before any conviction or judgment against the persons upon whom the same were to be levied.

---

19 Adams and Stephens, *Select Documents of English Constitutional History*, 44-47.

All which are utterly and directly contrary to the known laws and statutes and freedom of this realm.... And thereupon the said lords spiritual and temporal and commons pursuant to their respective letters and elections being now assembled in a full and free representative of this nation, taking into their most serious consideration the best means for attaining the ends aforesaid, do in the first place (as their ancestors in like case have usually done) for the vindicating and asserting their ancient rights and liberties, declare:

That the pretended power of suspending of laws or the execution of laws by regal authority without consent of parliament is illegal.

That the pretended power of dispensing with laws, or the execution of laws, by regal authority, as it hath been assumed and exercised of law, is illegal.

That the commission for erecting the late court of commissioners for ecclesiastical causes and all other commissions and courts of like nature are illegal and pernicious.

That the levying money for or to the use of the crown by pretence of prerogative without grant of parliament for a longer time or in other manner than the same is or shall be granted is illegal.

That it is the right of the subjects to petition the king and all commitments and prosecutions for such petitioning are illegal.

That the raising or keeping a standing army within the kingdom in time of peace unless it be with consent of parliament is against law.

That the subjects which are Protestants may have arms for their defence suitable to their conditions and as allowed by law.

That election of members of parliament ought to be free.

That the freedom of speech and debates or proceedings in parliament ought not to be impeached or questioned in any court or place out of parliament.

That excessive bail ought not to be required nor excessive fines imposed nor cruel and unusual punishments inflicted.

That jurors ought to be duly impanelled and returned and jurors which pass upon men in trials for high treason ought to be freeholders.

That all grants and promises of fines and forfeitures of particular persons before conviction are illegal and void.

And that for redress of all grievances and for the amending, strengthening and preserving of the laws parliaments ought to be held frequently.

And they do claim, demand and insist upon all and singular the premises as their undoubted rights and liberties and that no declarations, judgments, doings or proceedings to the prejudice of the people in any of the said premises ought in any wise to be drawn hereafter into consequence or example....

Finally, a look at the American Bill of Rights, the first ten amendments to the U.S. Constitution, demonstrates the heritage our Founders received from ancient English law:

THE AMERICAN BILL OF RIGHTS[20]

Article I

Freedom of Religion, of Speech, of the Press, and Right of Petition. "Congress shall make no law respecting an establishment of religion, or prohibiting the free exercise thereof; or abridging the freedom of speech, or of the press; or the right of the people peaceably to assemble, and to petition the Government for a redress of grievances."

Article II

Right of People to Bear Arms and not to be Infringed. "A well regulated Militia, being necessary to the security of a free State, the right of the people to keep and bear Arms, shall not be infringed by law."

Article III

Quartering of Troops. "No Soldier shall, in time of peace be quartered in any house, without the consent of the Owner, nor in time of war, but in a manner to be prescribed by law."

Article IV

Persons and House to be Secure from Unreasonable Searches and Seizures. "The right of the people to be secure in their persons, houses, papers, and effects, against unreasonable searches and seizures, shall not be violated, and no Warrant shall issue, but upon probable cause, supported by Oath or affirmation, and particularly describing the place to be searched, and the persons or things to be seized."

Article V

Trials for Crime—Just Compensation for Private Property Taken for Public Use. "No person shall be held to answer for a capital, or otherwise infamous crime, unless on a presentment of indictment of a Grand Jury, except in cases arising in the land or naval forces, or in the Militia, when in actual service, in time of War or public danger; nor shall any person be subject for the same offence to be twice put in jeopardy of life or limb; nor shall be compelled in any criminal case to be a witness against himself, nor be deprived of life, liberty, or property, without due process of law; nor shall private property be taken for public use without just compensation."

Article VI

Civil Rights in Trials for Crimes Enumerated. "In all criminal prosecutions, the accused shall enjoy the right to a speedy and public trial, by an impartial jury of the State and district wherein the crime shall have been committed, which district shall have been previously ascertained by law, and to be informed of the nature and cause of the accusation; to be confronted with the witnesses against him; to have compulsory process for obtaining witnesses in his favor, and to have the Assistance of Counsel for his defense."

Article VII

Preservation of Right of Trial by Jury. "In suits at common law, where the value in controversy shall exceed twenty dollars, the right of trial by jury shall be preserved, and no fact tried by a jury, shall be otherwise re-examined in any Court of the United States, than according to the rules of the common law."

---

20 Slater, *T&L*, 349-350.

Article VIII

Excessive Bail, Fines and Punishments Prohibited. "Excessive bail shall not be required, nor excessive fines imposed, nor cruel and unusual punishments inflicted."

Article IX

Reserved Right of People. "The enumeration in the Constitution, of certain rights, shall not be construed to deny or disparage others retained by the people."

Article X

Powers Not Delegated, Reserved to States and People Respectively. "The powers not delegated to the United States by the Constitution, nor prohibited by it to the States, are reserved to the States respectively, or to the people."

Discuss the chart of the progression of liberty through these four documents. Then we will compare them with the American Bill of Rights.

As a student, which of the rights listed in the American Bill of Rights are most important to you and affect your life today? List them in the order of their importance to you.

Liberties from Magna Charta to American Bill of Rights

Document	Magna Charta	Petition of Right	English Bill of Rights	American Bill of Rights
Date and Context	1215 King John forced by barons to sign charter of specified liberties	1628 Charles I restated the rights of the Magna Charta	1689 Outlining for William and Mary, new monarchs, the rights of Englishmen	1791 After the ratification of the U.S. Constitution, the Bill of Rights was the first ten amendments
Liberties	• Habeas corpus • Trial by Jury • Due Process	Limited: • Taxation • Billeting of soldiers • Imprisonment without cause • Use of martial law	• Created separation of powers • Limited powers of the king and queen • Enhanced democratic election • Bolstered freedom of speech	• Guarantees of personal freedoms and rights • Clearly limits the government's power • Explicitly declares that all powers not specifically delegated to Congress by the Constitution are reserved for the states or the people

Christian Philosophers of Constitutional Government

John Locke 1632–1704[21]

During the seventeenth and eighteenth centuries many Christians were searching the Scriptures for a form of government. There were questions of great concern to be settled—for instance, did kings have divine authority for all they did especially the evil? The questions of a law of nations, the Scriptural basis for a commonwealth or a republic, concern for the separation of the powers of government,—all these and more were the subject of study for many scholars.

Among those who were most influential upon American Constitutional government was John Locke—a Christian philosopher read by the Founding Father clergy and by the men, women, and children of the American Revolution. The work that was most influential upon American Constitutional government was his *Second Essay on Civil Government*. A reproduction of the 1714 edition can be found on pages 57–125 of *The Christian History of the Constitution*.

John Locke can justly be described as one of the most brilliant of political writers. Two years after the Glorious Revolution of 1688, Locke published "Two Treatises on Government" in which he successfully vindicated the principles upon which the revolution was founded. In these essays he refuted the doctrine of the Divine Right of Kings as being contrary to God's law.

John Locke was widely read in America by the clergy and by the Founding Fathers. His development of political theory was found in many of the sermons, newspapers, and educational writing of the period for about seventy-five years preceding the American Christian Revolution. His recognition of the internal sovereignty of Christianity is expressed in the following statement: *"As men we have God for our King, and are under the Law of Reason: as Christians, we have Jesus the Messiah for our King, and are under the Law reveal'd by him in the Gospel* [From "The Reasonableness of Christianity," 1695]."

LOCKE'S INFLUENCE[22]

Locke, in particular, was the authority to whom the Patriots paid greatest deference. He was the most famous of seventeenth century democratic theorists, and his ideas had their due weight with the colonists. Almost every writer seems to have been influenced by him, many quoted his words, and the argument of others shows the unmistakable imprint of his philosophy. The first great speech of Otis was wholly based upon Locke's ideas; Samuel Adams, on the "Rights of the Colonists as Men and as British Subjects," followed the same model. Many of the phrases of the Declaration of Independence may be found in Locke's Treatise; there is hardly any important writer of this time who does not openly refer to Locke, or tacitly follow the lead he

---

21 Slater, *T&L*, 175.
22 Hall, *CHOC I*, 51.

had taken. The argument in regard to the limitations upon Parliament was taken from Locke's reflections on the "supreme legislature" and the necessary restrictions upon its authority. No one stated more strongly than did he the basis for the doctrine that "taxation without representation is tyranny." No better epitome of the Revolutionary theory could be found than in John Locke on civil government [C. Edward Merriam, *A History of American Political Theories*, New York: Macmillan Company, 1903, 90]."

John Locke and the American Christian Constitution[23]

For one hundred and fifty years prior to the American Revolution the Colonists studied the Scriptures for the authority and source of government. They regarded the Bible as their *"Political Textbook"*. From the pulpit and the rostrum the clergy preached political principles based upon their studies of writers who believed that government should be *revelational of God*.

In a study entitled *The New England Clergy and the American Revolution*, Alice Baldwin indicates the degree to which the clergy educated the colonists in the Scriptural principles of government and of the quality of their knowledge and involvement in the political life of the new nation:

The New England clergy of the eighteenth century occupied a position of peculiar influence and power in the life of their own communities and of the several colonies.… They were for the most part a 'learned clergy', graduates of Harvard or of Yale.… They preached not only on Sunday but on many special occasions prescribed by the churches or ordered by the colonial assemblies, such as days of fasting and prayer and days of thanksgiving.… The sources from which the New England ministers developed their theories may be learned partly from the quotations and foot-notes which frequently are to be found in sermons and pamphlets, partly from diaries, letters, and other documents.… The most common source was the Bible.… Indeed there was never a principle derived from more secular reading that was not strengthened and sanctified by the Scriptures …

The next great source was the works of John Locke, his essays on religious toleration and human understanding as well as those on government. He was quoted by name as early as 1738, but his influence is to be seen in earlier works. Especially after 1763 the references to him are numerous, not only by the more prominent ministers of the larger towns but by those of the country villages as well."

For many years there has been a concerted effort to separate Christians from John Locke. He has been called a Deist, classified as a philosopher of the French Revolution, and appropriated by the Progressive Educators. Now, through the documentation of the *primary sources,* referred to by Miss Baldwin, the *Christian History of the Constitution,* compiled by Verna M. Hall, reveals him as a *saved Christian.*

In the fifth edition of *A Commonplace-Book to the Holy Bible: or the Scripture's Sufficiency Practically Demonstrated,* by John Locke and published by the American Tract Society, there occurs the following statement:

A relative having inquired of Mr. Locke what was the shortest and surest way for a young gentleman to attain a true knowledge of the Christian religion, he replied in these golden words: 'Let him study the Holy Scripture, especially in the New Testament. Therein are contained the words of eternal life. It has God for its Author, Salvation for its end, and Truth without any mixture of error for its matter'

The study of the *original* volumes of John Locke reveal his extensive marginal notes from Scripture. His Scriptural research and his political treatises were the axe which finally cut the root of the *Divine Right of Kings* theory of government. In America he was widely studied and his phrases and statements can be found interlaced and quoted in the writings of our Founders.

"John Locke, the Philosopher of the American Revolution "was admitted to Christ Church College in 1651, when Dr. Owen, the Independent was Dean,—the same who was thought of for the presidency of Harvard

---

[23] Slater, *T&L*, 353-354

College. 'Educated,' says Sir James, 'among the English Dissenters, during the short period of their political ascendency, he early imbibed *the deep piety and ardent spirit of liberty which actuated that body of men.... "By the Independent divines, who were his instructors, our philosopher was taught those principles of religious liberty which they were the first to disclose to the world* ["The Pulpit of the American Revolution" by John Wingate Thornton, 1860]."

> What descriptive title best describes John Locke's contribution to the American Revolution? What is the title of his most important work for Americans?

> Why is it so important that John Locke finally destroyed the unbiblical idea of the "Divine Right of Kings"?

Charles de Montesquieu 1689–1755

Although Montesquieu was a Frenchman he spent many years in the study of the British Constitutional system of government. He was one of the philosophers read by our Founding Fathers. His work *The Spirit of Laws* is founded upon a conviction shared by the Christian philosophers, namely, that because God rules His universe by unchangeable laws, governments should be ruled by laws and not by men. Montesquieu recognized that Christianity must be the basis of government and its laws—not changeable society.

Montesquieu sought to identify the functions of the legislative, executive, and judicial powers in government and saw them as providing a necessary system of check and balance upon each other.

THE SPIRIT OF LAWS[24]
BOOK 1: OF LAWS IN GENERAL

"1.—Of the Relation of Laws to Different Beings

"LAWS, in their most general signification, are the necessary relations arising from the nature of things. In this sense all beings have their laws: the Deity His laws, the material world its laws, the intelligences superior to man their laws, the beasts their laws, man his laws.

"They who assert that a blind fatality produced the various effects we behold in this world talk very absurdly; for can any thing be more unreasonable than to pretend that a blind fatality could be productive of intelligent beings?

"There is, then, a prime reason; and laws are the relations subsisting between it and different beings, and the relations of these to one another.

"God is related to the universe, as Creator and Preserver; the laws by which He created all things are those by which He preserves them. He acts according to these rules, because He knows them; He knows them, because He made them; and He made them, because they are in relation of his Wisdom and power...."

---

24 Hall, *CHOC I*, 134-138

Part IV: The Impact of Christ on Religion, Education, and Government

BOOK XI,
"OF THE LAWS WHICH ESTABLISH POLITICAL LIBERTY WITH REGARD TO THE CONSTITUTION"

"6.—Of the Constitution of England

"In every government there are three sorts of power: the legislative; the executive in respect to things dependent on the law of nations; and the executive in regard to matters that depend on the civil law.

"By virtue of the first, the prince or magistrate enacts temporary or perpetual laws, and amends or abrogates those that have already been enacted. By the second, he makes peace or war, sends or receives embassies, establishes the public security, and provides against invasions. By the third, he punishes criminals, or determines the disputes that arise between individuals. The latter we shall call the judiciary power, and the other simply the executive power of the state.

"The political liberty of the subject is a tranquillity of mind arising from the opinion each person has of his safety. In order to have this liberty, it is requisite the government be so constituted as one man need not be afraid of another.

"When the legislative and executive powers are united in the same person, or in the same body of magistrates, there can be no liberty; because apprehensions may arise, lest the same monarch or senate should enact tyrannical laws, to execute them in a tyrannical manner.

"Again, there is no liberty, if the judiciary power be not separated from the legislative and executive. Were it joined with the legislative, the life and liberty of the subject would be exposed to arbitrary control; for the judge would be then the legislator. Were it joined to the executive power, the judge might behave with violence and oppression.

"There would be an end of everything, were the same man or the same body, whether of the nobles or of the people, to exercise those three powers, that of enacting laws, that of executing the public resolutions, and of trying the causes of individuals....

"Hence it is that many of the princes of Europe, whose aim has been levelled at arbitrary power, have constantly set out with uniting in their own persons all the branches of magistracy, and all the great offices of state....

"As in a country of liberty, every man who is supposed a free agent ought to be his own governor; the legislative power should reside in the whole body of the people. But since this is impossible in large states, and in small ones is subject to many inconveniences, it is fit the people should transact by their representatives what they cannot transact by themselves [Charles de Secondat Montesquieu, *The Spirit of Laws*, 1748, rev. ed., trans., Thomas Nugent, New York: The Colonial Press, 1900, 1: 147, 151–152, 153, 154–156, 157–158, 159–160]."

As Christian educators we note with interest his statement relating education and the principles of government, indicating their inseparability: "That the Laws of Education ought to be relative to the Principles of Government."

Montesquieu, as did Locke, relates law to its primary source—God. In his opening statement of *The Spirit of Laws* he states: "God is related to the universe, as Creator and Preserver; the laws by which He created all things are those by which He preserves them."

What was Montesquieu's great work? He provided us with valuable reflections on the three branches of government; list them in your notebook.

William Blackstone 1723-1780

We have already indicated that Blackstone was important to Englishmen by his publication in 1765 of *Commentaries on the Laws of England* which represented the first collection of the common law of England. This became the book which American lawyers of the eighteenth and nineteenth centuries studied in order to become familiar with the English conception of law or Common Law.

As we have witnessed in the twentieth century a decline in the knowledge and understanding of American Constitutional law, so has Blackstone become unfamiliar to American lawyers and has been missing from their education.

"§ 39. 3. Law of nature.—This will of his Maker is called the law of nature. For as God, when He created matter, and endued it with a principle of mobility, established certain rules for the perpetual direction of that motion; so, when He created man, and endued him with <u>free will to conduct himself in all parts of life, He laid down certain immutable laws of human nature,</u> whereby that free will is in some degree regulated and restrained, and gave him also the faculty of reason to discover the purport of those laws.

"Considering the Creator only a Being of infinite *power*, He was able unquestionably to have prescribed whatever laws He pleased to His creature, man, however unjust or severe. But as He is also a Being of infinite *wisdom*, He has laid down only such laws as were founded in those relations of justice, that existed in the nature of things antecedent to any positive precept. <u>These are the eternal, immutable laws of good and evil,</u> to which the Creator Himself in all his Dispensations conforms; and which He has enabled human reason to discover, so far as they are necessary for the conduct of human actions. Such, among others, are these principles: that we should live honestly, should hurt nobody, and should render to everyone his due; to which three general precepts Justinian has reduced the whole doctrine of law.

"But if the discovery of these first principles of the <u>law of nature depended</u> only upon the <u>due exertion of right reason</u>, and could not otherwise be obtained than by a chain of metaphysical disquisitions, mankind would have wanted some inducement to have quickened their inquiries, and the greater part of the world would have rested content in mental indolence, and ignorance its inseparable companion. As, therefore, the Creator is a Being, not only of infinite *power*, and *wisdom*, but also of infinite *goodness*, He has been pleased so to contrive the constitution and frame of humanity, that we should want no other prompter than to inquire after and pursue the rule of right, but only our own self-love, that universal principle of action.

"For He has so intimately connected, so inseparably interwoven the laws of eternal justice with <u>the happiness of each individual</u>, that the latter cannot be attained but by observing the former; and, if the former be punctually obeyed, it cannot but induce the latter. In consequence of which mutual connection of justice and human felicity, He has not perplexed the law of nature with a multitude of abstracted rules and precepts, referring merely to the fitness or unfitness of things, as some have vainly surmised; but has graciously reduced the rule of obedience to this one paternal precept, "that man should pursue his own true and substantial happiness." This is the foundation of what we call ethics, or <u>natural law.</u> For the several articles into which it is branched in our systems, amount to no more than demonstrating, that this or that action

---

25 Hall. *CHOC I*, 140-146.

tends to man's real happiness, and therefore very justly concluding that the performance of it is a part of the law of nature; or, on the other hand, that this or that action is destructive to man's real happiness, and therefore that the law of nature forbids it.

"This law of nature, being coeval with mankind and dictated by God Himself, is of course superior in obligation to any other. It is binding over all the globe in all countries, and at all times: no human laws are of any validity, if contrary to this; and such of them as are valid derive all their force, and all their authority, mediately or immediately, from this original.

But in order to apply this to the particular exigencies of each individual, it is still necessary to have recourse to human reason: whose office it is to discover, as was before observed, what the law of nature directs in every circumstance of life; by considering, what method will tend most effectually to our own substantial happiness. And if our reason were always, as in our first ancestor before his transgression, clear and perfect, unruffled by passions, unclouded by prejudice, unimpaired by disease or intemperance, the task would be pleasant and easy; we should need no other guide but this. But every man now finds the contrary in his own experience; that his reason is corrupt, and his understanding full of ignorance and error.

"§ 40. 4 Revealed Law.—This has given manifold occasion for the benign interposition of divine providence; which, in compassion to the frailty, the imperfection, and the blindness of human reason hath been pleased, at sundry times and in divers manners, to discover and enforce its laws by an immediate and direct revelation. The doctrines thus delivered we call the <u>revealed or divine law, and they are to be found only in the Holy Scriptures.</u> These precepts, when revealed, are found upon comparison to be really a part of the original law of nature, as they tend in all their consequences to man's felicity. But we are not from thence to conclude that the knowledge of these truths was attainable by reason, in its present corrupted state; since we find that, until they were revealed, they were hid from the wisdom of the ages. As then the moral precepts of this law are indeed of the same original with those of the law of nature, so their intrinsic obligation is of equal strength and perpetuity. Yet undoubtedly <u>the revealed law is of infinitely more authenticity than that moral system, which is framed by ethical writers, and denominated the natural law.</u> Because one is the law of nature, expressly declared so to be by God Himself; the other is only what, by the assistance of human reason, we imagine to be that law. If we could be as certain of the latter as we are of the former, both would have an equal authority; but, till then, they can never be put in any competition together.

"<u>Upon these two foundations, the law of nature and the law of revelation, depend all human laws;</u> that is to say, no human laws should be suffered to contradict these."[26]

---

26 Hall, *CHOC I*, 141.

BIOGRAPHY OF BLACKSTONE

"AMONG those who have risen to eminence by the profession of the law, none have obtained a more extended and durable reputation than Sir William Blackstone….

"He seems from the first to have made up his mind to follow the profession of the law, …

"At Oxford he had diligently progressed in the study of the classics, mathematics, &c.; before he was twenty, had compiled a Treatise on the Elements of Architecture, …

"… In 1750, he took his degree of Doctor on Civil Law, and thereby became a member of the convocation….

"He formed the design of reducing into system the common law, which had hitherto lain in scattered fragments in the reports, or in large masses in the Institutes of Coke, …—of treating with elegance a subject on which the graces of composition had never before been bestowed—of teaching, in a place where it had never before been taught, a science which no one there desired to learn.… Too much gratitude cannot be paid to him by lawyers, for this gratuitous and invaluable present to his profession.

"… [I]n 1765 appeared the first volume of the Commentaries.… It may be inferred from what has been said, that he was no enthusiast either in religion or in politics; in the former he was a sincere believer in Christianity, from a profound investigation of its evidences; in the latter he was what would be called a Conservative, friendly to mild but authoritative government, inimical to the agitations of pretended patriots [W. N. Welsby ed., *Lives of Eminent English Judges of the Seventeenth and Eighteenth Centuries*, Philadelphia, PA: T. & J. W. Johnson, 1846, 139, 332, 334, 335, 337, 338, 339, 340–341, 347, 357].

"In 1765 Blackstone published his *Commentaries on the Laws of England*. This study represented the first collection of the common law of England with detailed explanations as to how this law functioned specifically in a constitutional monarchy—with its heritage of Magna Charta, Petition of Right and the Bill of Rights. This digest of English common law represented also a remarkable commentary on the philosophy of law, particularly as it related to the rights of individuals in society. Blackstone is specific and detailed in his analysis, and thus became a basic part of the study of the course of Law by English and American students.

"Lawyers who had 'read law' had read Coke's *Institutes,* published between 1628 and 1644, the authoritative systematic exposition of the common law down to Blackstone's *Commentaries,* published 1765–69. Thus they were brought up on ideas of 'the law of the land,' of the immemorial rights of Englishmen guaranteed by Magna Carta. Blackstone at once became the first book to be studied by American lawyers and held that place till the beginning of the present century. The *Commentaries* had an exceptionally large sale in the colonies. We are told that twenty-five hundred copies were bought in America before the Revolution. A subscription reprint was published in Philadelphia in 1771–72. The list of subscribers is headed by 'John Adams, Esq, barrister at law, Boston'. Blackstone set forth Coke's doctrine in readable form."

"Blackstone, as did Locke, defined the Law of Nature as 'will of his Maker.'

"Thus we find, through *Locke, Montesquieu* and *Blackstone,* the establishment of a Christian philosophy of government and law, which aided our American colonists to write an American Christian Constitution [Roscoe Pound, *The Development of Constitutional Guarantees of Liberty*].

Blackstone with Locke and other Christians identified the Law of Nature as God's Law and indicated that human law must not contradict either the Law of Nature or the divine law which we find revealed in Holy Scriptures.[27]

---

27 Slater, *T&L*, 176.

> POLITICAL FREEDOM AS THE WESTERN WORLD HAS KNOWN IT,
> IS ONLY A POLITICAL READING OF THE BIBLE.
> WHITTAKER CHAMBERS

William Blackstone can be called the authority on what? What was Blackstone's most famous work, widely studied by American lawyers?

Explain this quote in your own words: "This law of nature, being coeval (having the same age or date of origin) with mankind and dictated by God Himself, is of course superior in obligation to any other. It is binding over all the globe in all countries, and at all times: no human laws are of any validity, if contrary to this; and such of them as are valid derive all their force, and all their authority, mediately or immediately, from this original."

Record the most significant ideas contributed by Locke, Montesquieu, and Blackstone to the "idea of America."

Locke	Montesquieu	Blackstone

Now we have come to the conclusion of our study of the Reformation. Can you clearly explain both natural and revealed law?

How did the reform of religion, education, law and government affect the founding of America?

Part IV Essay

Write a formal essay thoroughly explaining the two questions above.

Nation Makers

Part V:
America–The Fullest Expression of a Christian Nation

- America; the Fullest Expression of Christianity
- Legacy of Parent Colonies
- Theology of the American Republic
- Restoring the Republic

America–The Fullest Expression of a Christian Nation

Because God moves history forward by ideas, the "idea of America" as a full expression of the Christian government, self and civil, has a unique role and purpose in God's providence. We are not like other nations. When fully understood, the "idea of America" is dazzling in its nobility and scope, in its eternal principles, and in its truth, goodness, and beauty.

We are privileged to live at such a time in history to experience the blessings of self-government and the liberty granted to us by God's grace.

We have come to the final chapter of our study of *Nation Makers* of the American Republic. We have studied in depth the themes that comprise the "idea of America:"

- The Character of Liberty
- The Principle of Individuality
- God's Hand in History
- Natural and Revealed Law
- The Impact of Christ on Religion, on Education, and on Government

The culminating link on the Chain of Christianity® is the founding of a Constitutional Republic in America—the fullest expression of a Christian nation in the history of the world.

This final chapter of our study examines the nature of the union that brought forth a nation—the legacy of the parent colonies and the theology of the American Republic—the two ingredients that cemented our union.

The Parent Colonies, "the two provinces of Virginia and New England . . . may be considered as the original and parent colonies; in imitation of which . . . all the others have been successively planted and reared."[1]

The legacy left to us by the Parent Colonies is the product of the theology that formed the knowledge of God and His Word preached from the pulpits for 200 years and meticulously taught in the universities as it applies to all of life: the theology of the Reformation.

This legacy is the essence of the "idea of America" and her exceptionalism—her unique nature and purpose among nations.

---

1 Hall, *CHOC I*, 276

ORIGINAL AND PARENT COLONIES

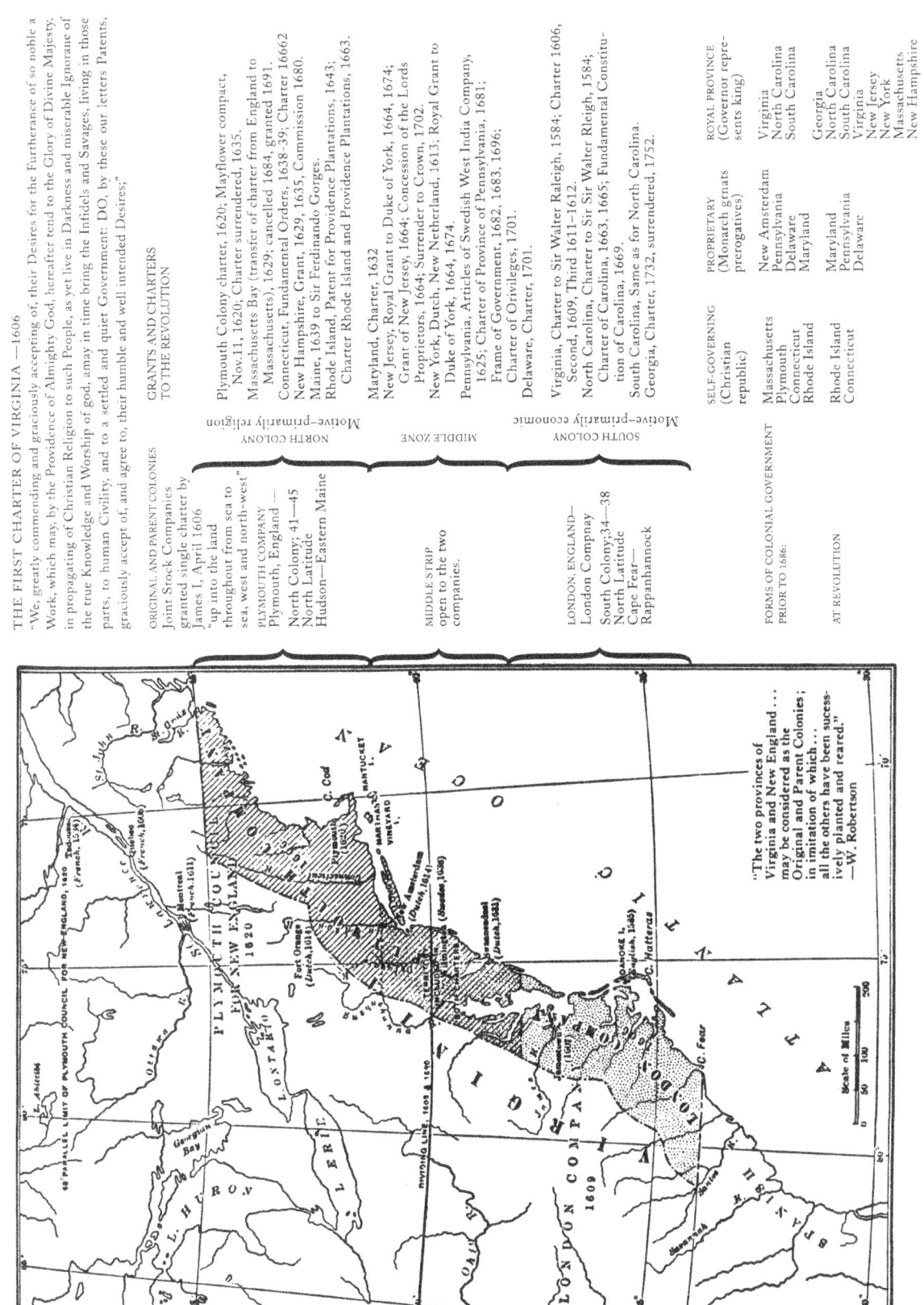

"The two provinces of Virginia and New England... may be considered as the Original and Parent Colonies; in imitation of which... all the others have been successively planted and reared." —W. Robertson

THE FIRST CHARTER OF VIRGINIA —1606

"We, greatly commending and graciously accepting of, their Desires for the Furtherance of so noble a Work, which may, by the Providence of Almighty God, hereafter tend to the Glory of Divine Majesty, in propagating of Christian Religion to such People, as yet live in Darkness and miserable Ignorance of the true Knowledge and Worship of god, amay in time bring the Infidels and Savages, living in those parts, to human Civility, and to a settled and quiet Government: DO, by these our letters Patents, graciously accept of, and agree to, their humble and well intended Desires;"

ORIGINAL AND PARENT COLONIES
Joint Stock Companies granted single charter by James I, April 1606 "up into the land throughout from sea to sea, west and north-west"

PLYMOUTH COMPANY
Plymouth, England —
North Colony; 41—45 North Latitude
Hudson—Eastern Maine

NORTH COLONY — Motive—primarily religion

MIDDLE STRIP
open to the two companies.

MIDDLE ZONE

LONDON, ENGLAND—
London Company
South Colony;34—38 North Latitude
Cape Fear—Rappahannock

SOUTH COLONY — Motive—primarily economic

GRANTS AND CHARTERS TO THE REVOLUTION

Plymouth Colony charter, 1620; Mayflower compact, Nov.11, 1620; Charter surrendered, 1635.
Massachusetts Bay (transfer of charter from England to Massachusetts), 1629; cancelled 1684, granted 1691.
Connecticut, Fundamental Orders, 1638-39; Charter 16662
New Hampshire, Grant, 1629, 1635, Commission 1680.
Maine, 1639 to Sir Ferdinando Gorges.
Rhode Island, Patent for Providence Plantations, 1643;
Charter Rhode Island and Providence Plantations, 1663.

Maryland, Charter, 1632
New Jersey, Royal Grant to Duke of York, 1664, 1674;
Grant of New Jersey, 1664; Concession of the Lords Proprietors, 1664; Surrender to Crown, 1702.
New York, Dutch, New Netherland, 1613; Royal Grant to Duke of York, 1664, 1674.
Pennsylvania, Articles of Swedish West India Company, 1625; Charter of Province of Pennsylvania, 1681; Frame of Government, 1682, 1683, 1696;
Charter of Orivileges, 1701.
Delaware, Charter, 1701.

Virginia, Charter to Sir Walter Raleigh, 1584; Charter 1606, Second, 1609, Third 1611-1612.
North Carolina, Charter to Sir Sir Walter Rleigh, 1584;
Charter of Carolina, 1663, 1665; Fundamental Constitution of Carolina, 1669.
South Carolina, Same as for North Carolina.
Georgia, Charter, 1732, surrendered, 1752.

FORMS OF COLONIAL GOVERNMENT PRIOR TO 1686:

SELF-GOVERNING (Christian republic)	PROPRIETARY (Monarch grnats prerogatives)	ROYAL PROVINCE (Governor represents king)
Massachusetts	New Amsterdam	Virginia
Plymouth	Pennsylvania	North Carolina
Connecticut	Delaware	South Carolina
Rhode Island	Maryland	

AT REVOLUTION

		Georgia
		North Carolina
	Maryland	South Carolina
Rhode Island	Pennsylvania	Virginia
Connecticut	Delaware	New Jersey
		New York
		Massachusetts
		New Hampshire

Part V: America; Fullest Expression of a Christian Nation

Virginia

The first charter for English colonization in America was granted by the crown, by Queen Elizabeth, in 1578. Soon after, Sir Walter Raleigh organized a squadron of small ships, led by Sir Richard Greenville, that landed and established a colony on the island of Roanoke which was then Virginia but is now North Carolina. The colony suffered "by famine, or by the unrelenting cruelty of those barbarians by whom they were surrounded," and disappeared completely by 1587.

Meanwhile, in England by 1606, interest in Virginia was renewed. James I divided the land that stretches from the thirty-fourth to the fifty-fifth degree of latitude, into two districts, one called the south colony of Virginia and one called the north colony. Proprietors outfitted ships in 1606 under the command of Captain Newport and sailed for the new world.

The Burning of James Towne by Howard Pyle

James Towne 1607

On April 26, 1607 after an unusually long voyage of 144 days, the 3 ships and 105 men and boys made landfall at the southern edge of the mouth of the Chesapeake Bay at the Atlantic Ocean. They named the location Cape Henry.

There, Pastor Robert Hunt planted a cross and led a dedication service where all of Virginia –America – was dedicated to God.

Within a few weeks, the settlers chose a permanent inland site for their colony on the James River, naming it James Towne in honor of King James I.

As one of the two original, Parent Colonies, setting a pattern that other colonists imitated, Virginia was settled as a royal province. Virginia was established for commercial enterprise and "the enriching of commerce by new commodities". The Virginia charter declared the intention to "tend to the Glory of his Divine Majesty, in propagating of Christian Religion" to people ignorant of the true knowledge and worship of God.

The Jamestown colony suffered calamities, sickness, famine, martial law, Indian massacres, and hardships. John Smith and other leaders led the colonists through the difficulties, and Jamestown has the distinction of being the first permanent English colony in America.

Representation

The Virginia colony transplanted the seed of **representative government** as a direct continuation of English society and custom. In fact, the seed of monarchical government here introduced, long influenced the development of her history and accounts for many struggles against the truer strain of Christian self-government representing all men. The Virginians were Royalists, members of the Established Church of England—and thus firm supporters of church and state.

As Englishmen, the Virginians were accustomed to certain rights and privileges, among these the law-

John Smith's Map of Virginia

making or legislative function. Accordingly, in the year 1619, Sir George Yeardly called the **first legislative assembly held in Virginia.** This gave the Virginians the satisfaction of beholding among themselves an image of the English constitution, which they reverenced as the most perfect model of free government.

Virginia's episcopal form of church government produced the county system as the unit of representation for the individual in the civil government. The county system was more removed from the direct control of the entire population, as its offices were generally appointive and self-perpetuating.

The fertile land, moderate climate, and waterways that gave access to the interior, all supported the development of large plantations along the rivers. These plantations operated like little towns highly organized around their industry and doing commerce with England.

"A glance at the map of Virginia shows to what a remarkable degree it is intersected by navigable rivers. This fact made it possible for plantations, even at a long distance from the coast, to have each its own private wharf, where a ship from England could unload its cargo of tools, cloth, or furniture, and receive a cargo of tobacco in return. As the planters were thus supplied with most of the necessaries of life, there was no occasion for the kind of trade that builds up towns.

Part V: America; Fullest Expression of a Christian Nation

> "The Virginia system concentrating the administration of local affairs in the hands of a few county families, was eminently favorable for developing **skillful and vigorous leadership.** While in the history of Massachusetts during the revolution we are chiefly impressed with the wonderful degree in which the mass of the people exhibited the kind of political training that nothing in the world except the habit of parliamentary discussion can impart; on the other hand, Virginia at that time gave us – in Washington, Jefferson, Henry, Madison, and Marshall, to mention no others – such a group of consummate leaders as the world has seldom seen equaled (John Fiske's *Civil Government in the United States*, 1890)."[2]

As the impact of the Reformation in education and government permeated formal schooling and preaching in Virginia pulpits, Virginians deepened their grasp of Scripture as it formed in their thinking Biblical models of government and economics. They studied the writings of Reformation thinkers: Locke, Montesquieu, and Blackstone. They discussed and debated principles of liberty, as they wrestled with the governance of their colony until they came to unity. This unity bound them in spirit to the Puritans in Massachusetts in understanding God's gift of liberty.

It was a Virginian who wrote the Declaration of Independence. It was a Virginian who led the farmers and shopkeepers in forming "a continental army." It was a Virginian who purchased the Louisiana territory from Napoleon and sent explorers west to open the nation from sea to shining sea.

Virginia is the mother of eight American presidents: George Washington, Thomas Jefferson, James Madison, James Monroe, William Henry Harrison, Zachary Taylor, John Tyler, and Woodrow Wilson.

Discuss the major qualities of the Virginia Colony including the church, the culture, and the view of the Virginia colonists in relation to England. What happened in 1619 in Virginia and why is this significant?

THE SCHOOL FOR STATESMEN

Virginia gave leadership to the nation through its formative years causing historians to consider how such a great generation of leaders came about. It was no curious historical accident that so many men of remarkable capacity should emerge at this particular time. What forces molded their thinking and shaped their characters to prepare them to solve problems that were previously unsolvable in the history of the world? Most importantly, what can we learn from this great generation of leaders?

"There were three key ideas: First—scholarship for public service. Second—a period early in life where the scholarship was put into practice in a highly personal system, where the public servant would know his constituency on an individual basis. And third—the idea that if the country needs you to serve, you had no right to decline. While the Constitution has served us well, these three key ideas have unfortunately left our system. And if we wish to be worthy of our heritage, we mush renew this school for statesmen to insure that each American generation will have the leadership needed to maintain and improve the republic."[3]

The "Virginia system" emphasized scholarship for public service by the value of "things of the mind and spirit" centering on a classical education. It was considered fundamental to instill "a broad and generous way of thought and a deep and perceptive knowledge of earlier constructive civilizations" through the study of the classics. This large view of things and a broad understanding of men and nations included the knowledge of history, law and government.[4]

The structure of the county system imposed duties that formed the habit and skill of leadership. In the county, eight or more justices of the peace were appointed who must be men of "the best reputation, good governance and courage for the truth, men fearing God, not seeking the place for honor or conveniency … lovers of justice, judging the people equally and impartially". These justices constituted the county court and

---

2 Hall, *CHOC I*, 276-280
3 Dumas Malone and William H.B. Thomas, *A Miracle of Virginia: The School for Statesmen* (Ben Franklin Publishing of Charlottesville, 1984), 3.
4 Malone and Thomas, *A Miracle of Virginia: The School for Statesmen*, 41, 47.

had jurisdiction over civil and criminal matters.

County leaders might also have held the office of vestryman of the church parish, an office that included civil duties such as "seeing to the welfare of orphans and abandoned or illegitimate children; caring for the poor, the aged, and the sick; supervising the processioning of land; and dealing with public morals."[5]

Another county duty that forged leadership was that of militia officer responsible for the defense of the county.

Finally, service in the House of Burgesses, the lower branch of the General Assembly, was an avenue towards national leadership for Virginians. The men who became justices of the peace, vestrymen, militia officers, and later burgesses had early conditioning for posts of authority. Most importantly, these offices gave their county neighbors personal knowledge of their characters, their consciences, and their reliability.

The sense of obligation if called to serve the county or the nation in colonial Virginia was starkly different from the marketing for votes to gain places of power of today's political arena. Humility, sacrifice, and honor were the mark of the statesman. In his candidacy for a seat in the House of Delegates in 1777, James Madison was defeated as the result of his refusal to treat the voters with food and drink. It was Madison who fought for the stronger guarantee of freedom at the Virginia Constitutional Convention insisting on replacing the term "religious tolerance" with "the dictates of conscience."[6]

Perhaps that explains Jefferson's thought:

"When Benjamin Rush wrote Jefferson and asked, 'Who's the greatest man you know? You've been in France, you know Washington, Franklin; who of all the men you've met in the world is the greatest man?' Jefferson wrote back and said, 'That's an easy question to answer. James Madison is the greatest man in the world.' What did he mean? Well, I think that what he meant was that Madison was a man whose broad knowledge was coupled with a commitment of the ancient conception of virtue; Madison was incapable of acting unjustly."[7]

Finally, the leadership of Virginian statesmen continued for fifty crucial years:

"Even a superficial glance at the early history of the United States shows the Virginians were at the epicenter of the Constitutional process. The Constitutional Convention of 1787 was presided over by George Washington, whose almost silent but towering presence give stability and order to what might have otherwise been barroom brawl of quarrelsome colonies – almost independent nations – and the other Virginians moved within this framework to construct the final document and to make the Constitution work. Edmund Randolph backed by the whole Virginia delegation, carried Madison's Virginia Plan to the floor of the Constitutional Convention. The Virginia Plan was finally adopted, and moreover, the plan served as an agenda to systematically and relatively peacefully discuss the major questions of government. James Madison

The state's motto "Sic Semper Tyrannis" means "Thus Always to Tyrants." The seal was approved at Virginia's 1776 Constitutional Convention, and the principal designer is said to have been George Wythe.

---

5 Malone and Thomas, A Miracle of Virginia: *The School for Statesmen*, 22.
6 Malone and Thomas, A Miracle of Virginia: *The School for Statesmen*, 32.
7 Malone and Thomas, *A Miracle of Virginia: The School for Statesmen*, 59.

shepherded through the floor fights and compromises and was the most important leader in the national ratification struggles by the state conventions. Virginians carried the Constitution into practice; George Washington served two terms as the first President, his Attorney General was Randolph, and Thomas Jefferson his Secretary of State. After one stormy term with John Adams, the Virginia dynasty of Jefferson, Madison and Monroe carried the country through another six presidential terms of national leadership. In the same period, another Virginian, John Marshall, defined the powers and responsibilities of the Supreme Court. There was a period of fifty years from 1776, the year of both George Mason's Declaration of Rights in the Virginia Constitution and Jefferson's Declaration of Independence, to Jefferson's death on Independence Day, 1826, exactly fifty years after the Declaration, a period of fifty crucial years, during which Virginians carried the nation."[8]

Explain the two great contributions of Virginia to the founding of the nation: representation and statesmanship. Why are these models so important to Christian self-government?

"WHAT IS GOVERNMENT ITSELF, BUT THE GREATEST OF ALL REFLECTIONS ON HUMAN NATURE? IF MEN WERE ANGELS, NO GOVERNMENT WOULD BE NECESSARY. IF ANGELS WERE TO GOVERN MEN, NEITHER EXTERNAL NOR INTERNAL CONTROLS ON GOVERNMENT WOULD BE NECESSARY. IN FRAMING A GOVERNMENT WHICH IS TO BE ADMINISTERED BY MEN OVER MEN, THE GREAT DIFFICULTY LIES IN THIS: YOU MUST FIRST ENABLE THE GOVERNMENT TO CONTROL THE GOVERNED; AND IN THE NEXT PLACE OBLIGE IT TO CONTROL ITSELF."

JAMES MADISON, *THE FEDERALIST* NO. 51, FEBRUARY 8, 1788.

New England
The Pilgrims and the Puritans

Just thirteen years after the first settlers landed at James Towne, the Pilgrims sailed on the Mayflower to Plymouth Bay. Those who came to New England to form communities that became the Massachusetts colony were fleeing from persecution and oppression. What is the difference between the New England Puritans and the New England Pilgrims?

The Puritans were English Christians who demanded reformation of church and state by compulsion. They were bound to the Old Testament law and letter and refused to separate their own conscience from that of the national church. The Puritan believed that external law should be used to compel men to act in the right way. Puritans remained in the Church of England.

The Pilgrims were also English Christians. In contrast to the Puritans, they were willing to separate from the Church of England and regarded the "ecclesiastico-political institution" as incompatible with the New Testament church of Christ. The Pilgrim recognized that liberty was internal and came from God and not from government.

---

8 Malone and Thomas, *A Miracle of Virginia: The School for Statesmen*, 63-64.

The Pilgrims were the first settlers to come to New England in 1620. The story of their undertaking began with violent persecution in England that caused them to take refuge in Holland. They were farmers and some were trained in English universities, but all were students of the Bible, earnest believers in Christ, and shared a vision of an independent church.

The story of the exile in Holland, the voyage on the Mayflower, the hardships, sickness, death, labor, famine, and distresses they experienced is well known.

The Pilgrim Separatists established the beginnings of the Christian Republic in two major ways: first, their practice of **self-government** that became a model for the nation, and their **Christian character** well documented by their governor, William Bradford, in his *History of Plimoth Plantation*.

John Robinson sending the Pilgrims to America

"Fleeing both ecclesiastical and civil tyranny, the valiant Pilgrims of Plymouth Plantation brought to these shores Primitive Christianity. Like their counterparts of the first century of Christianity, they witnessed by their lives the consistency of their faith. Not one went back. In the record of Plymouth Colony we find the parenthood of our Republic. Here can be found the seed of all our important institutions. Here begins our precious record of *Christian Character, Christian Self-Government, Christian Economics, Christian Education* and *Biblical Christian Unity*. For it is what constitutes the character of individual Americans that determines whether our government, economics, education and unity are Christian or pagan."

CHRISTIAN SELF-GOVERNMENT

"New England's Congregational form of church government—local self-government of the church—was expressed also in the society. Each local township was a 'small, self-governing republic.'

"Of the various kinds of government to be found in the United States, we may begin by considering that of the New England township . . . It is in principle of all known forms of government the oldest as well as the simplest . . . In a New England township the people directly govern themselves; this government is the people . . . Jefferson said, 'Those wards, called townships in New England, are the vital principles of their governments, and have proved themselves the wisest invention ever devised by the wit of men for the perfect exercise of self-government, and for its preservation.'[9]

---

9 R.J. Slater, *T&L*, 178.

The First Document of Self-Government: The Mayflower Compact

John Elliot, the first missionary among the Indians

The tradition of Christian self-government was carried and documented on the Mayflower and culminated in America's first document of Christian self-government—*the Mayflower Compact.*

The purpose of the Compact, expressed in its original wording, was "to covenant and combine ourselves together into a civil body politic, for our better ordering and preserving and furtherance of the ends aforesaid; and by virtue hereof to enact, constitute, and frame such just and equal laws, ordinances, acts, constitutions, and offices, from time to time, as shall be thought most meet and convenient for the general good of the colony, unto which we promise due submission and obedience . . . solemnly and mutually in the presence of God, and one of another . . ."[10]

Plymouth Colony and American Christian Character

We come now to the precious record of America's Christian character. This record should be important to all Americans. It should be of particular importance to all American Christians. The ten-year period of the record of the Plymouth Colony from 1620–1630 presents a testimony of Pilgrim character, forged upon the anvil of the many hardships and temptations which beset them and threatened to wipe out their record. But God has a purpose here with these, His people. This history can be read in *The Christian History of the Constitution*, Vol. I pages 185–240. The account highlights the character of the Pilgrims:

    Faith and Steadfastness—pages 215–219

    Brotherly Love and Christian Care—pages 219–221

    Diligence and Industry—pages 221–223

    Liberty of Conscience—page 224

Explain the two great contributions of New England to the founding of the nation: Christian character and self-government. Why are they so important?

---

10 R.J. Slater, *T&L*, 179.

The Theology of the American Republic

William Ames

The Reformation of education begun by Peter Ramus led to clear thinking in every area of knowledge. This opened the way for a reformed thinker and master of Ramean reforms to produce the masterwork of theology that was taught as the "queen of the sciences" in American universities and churches for nearly 200 years. This book is *The Marrow of Sacred Divinity* and the writer is William Ames.

Puritan William Ames was born four years after Peter Ramus' murder and during the religious battles in England that shed quantities of martyr blood. As a student at Cambridge he sat under the teaching of William Perkins, known as the father of Puritanism. Ames became a master of Ramism and produced his book *Technometry* using the Ramean method of teaching and learning.

Shut out by the Anglicans, he exiled to Holland where he joined a colony of religious refugees, becoming a leader and a tutor, leading to the writing of *The Marrow of Theology* as a manual of Reformed theology for use with his students. His theology presented a practical divinity—the doctrine of "living to God."[11]

Ames saw all learning having its source in the mind of God from the initial idea of creation to the "sciences"—the subjects. He taught that the goal of all learning, the goal of every one of the "sciences," is "Eupraxia" or good action. In other words, the source of all learning is God and the end of all learning is doing His will.

He taught that the six arts that perfect the whole man are (1) logic, directing the intellect, (2) theology, the will, (3) grammar, (4) rhetoric, (5) math and (6) physics. Ames' technometry (method of organizing ideas in charts) to learn theology was employed for 150 years in American universities making goodness, "Eupraxia", the hallmark of American education.[12]

William Ames called theology the "queen of the sciences, a designation appropriate for a new nation whose king is Jesus."[13] Although Ames did not come to America, he knew the Pilgrims in Holland and spent time in the company of John Robinson, Pilgrim pastor. After his death, his wife and children travelled to Plymouth.[14] *The Marrow of Divinity* was welcomed and studied in the New England colony. *Marrow* became the theology textbook at Yale and Harvard. A close look at Ames' work shows that our Founding Fathers learned the first principles of government and the importance of Christian education from *The Marrow of Divinity*, the common curriculum of the American founding. Students actually memorized all of the *Marrow* and used the Ramean Method themselves to make their thinking clear and to fix it in their memory.

The theology documented by William Ames produced a good nation that became great. America was great because she was good.

---
11 William Ames, *The Marrow of Theology* (The Labyrinth Press, 1968), 77.
12 Ames, *The Marrow of Theology*, 78.
13 Rebecca H Beach and Carole G. Adams, "Finding the Real Common Core of American Christian Education: The Theology of American Librty" (speech, Reason for Hope, Virginia, Virginia Beach, February 11, 2015).
14 For further study of William Ames: Sprunger, Keith L. *The Learned Doctor William Ames: Dutch Backgrounds of English and American Puritanism.* Chicago: University of Illinois Press, 1972.

William Ames is the theologian of the American Christian Republic. The Ramean Method Ames employed in his *Marrow of Sacred Divinity*, diagramming complex ideas to make them easily understood, enabled the Founders to accomplish the unprecedented feat of unity with union that founded the Republic. That unity of thought and mind is the internal 'glue' of the Republic. Today, only a resurgence of Biblical-Christian learning and reasoning can restore and sustain the American Republic for future generations.

What is the goal and purpose of Ames' idea of education? What role did this play in colonial society?

What does "Eupraxia" mean and what does it have to do with learning?

How did the Ramean method of thinking employed in education enable the unity of the colonies in forming the Republic?

The Pastor, the Pulpit and American Liberty: Unity with Union

"The Christian church has been one of the most potent factors in the construction of the American Republic and one of the greatest bulwarks of its magnificent principles and institutions."[15]

The role of the pastor in the founding of America cannot be overstated. The many hours colonial Americans spent in church, as they faithfully honored the Sabbath in Virginia and in New England from the cradle to the grave, gave them a complete theological education. But beyond the centrality of the church in colonial life, the pastor imparted through teaching the Bible the spirit of Christian liberty, reverence for law, and faith in God.[16]

Pastors were involved in every aspect of public affairs making God's Word relevant to every situation that affected their communities. Their sermons, many hours long and printed to be read and re-read, stoked the fires of liberty and inculcated its principles in hearts and minds. The communities must reflect the model of Jesus Christ: "The divine love which shines out of His cross must be allowed to dominate all the affairs of human life … His manhood must be reproduced in our citizens, and the nation must wheel itself into line with the purposes of His coming kingdom of righteousness and peace and love."[8] The Colonial clergy were faithful to the whole counsel of God.

In the formative years of our nation, pastors preached Christ in politics, government, economics, and religion. Too many pastors today do not take a stand and have abandoned their responsibility to teach these subjects for fear of upsetting their people. The wealth of sermons of the Colonial clergy preserved to this day prove the absolute responsibility pastors took in serving their nation and their God. There are Election Sermons, Artillery Sermons, Fast Day Sermons, and many others demonstrating the extent to which pastors engaged the Gospel in every area of life.

At the call of service to the infant nation, pastors shed their robes and took up arms in the continental army to defeat the British. Many served in the legislature and considered that service equally important to their service in the pulpit at such a time. Pastors today have much to learn from the valiant and faithful pastors that formed the Republic in order to restore it to God's purpose.

We will look at two characters whose examples need emulation today: Rev. Samuel Davies and Rev. John Witherspoon.

---

15 Slater, *T&L*, 39.
16 Slater, *T&L*, 41.

Rev. Samuel Davies 1724-1761 — Virginia[17]

"Reverend Samuel Davies, for some time a pastor in Virginia, and afterwards President of Nassau Hall, deserves especial notice. He was born in Delaware, Nov. 3rd, 1724, and received his education in Pennsylvania. His grand characteristic, as a patriot and preacher, was **boldness**. This is a valuable attribute in every public agent. The great Lord Verulam declared, that 'if he were asked what is the first, second, and third thing necessary for success in business, he should answer, boldness, boldness, boldness.' **Timid and effeminate efforts in the pulpit are as inefficient and more destructive than elsewhere.** The stupid soul is startled into attention only by bold blows. Ministers may describe forever the beauties of nature, the pleasures of virtue, the dignity of self-respect and the vulgarity of vice, but until more exalted motives are urged, and more potent influences are employed, few effects will follow that are either great or good.

"Davies was the ablest Dissenter in the southern provinces. His custom was to study his discourses with great care. Being pressed to preach on a certain occasion without his usual preparation, he replied: 'It is a dreadful thing to talk nonsense in the name of the Lord.'

Davies' Defence of Religious Liberty

"But he was as prompt and fearless in any sudden emergency, as he was habitually deliberate and studious. Thanks to the movements in behalf of religious liberty made at the North, England granted the Toleration Act in favor of all the Colonies. Virginia, however, ruled by her Episcopal establishment, refused to admit that the Dissenters of their territory were included. Davies withstood all their forces alone, with Peyton Randolph at their head. **He had made himself a thorough master of English law, civil and ecclesiastical, and always chose to meet every persecuting indictment in the highest courts with his own plea.**

"Not satisfied with establishing his religious rights at the bar of colonial power, he went to England and obtained the explicit sanction of the highest authority with respect to the extension of the Toleration law to Virginia. It was during this mission that he gave another striking instance of his boldness. George II and many of his court were in the congregation of this American Dissenter. His majesty, struck with admiration, or forgetting the proprieties of the occasion, spoke several times to those around him and smiled. Davies paused a moment, and then looking sternly at the king, exclaimed, 'When the lion roars, the beasts of the forest all tremble; and when King Jesus speaks, the princes of earth should keep silence.'

"Mr. Davies was tall, manly and dignified. A distinguished character of the day, on seeing him pass, said: 'he looked like the ambassador of some great king.' His understanding was strong, his elocution graceful, and his address on some occasions was overwhelming. Patrick Henry was his neighbor and ardent admirer. It is believed that the renowned pupil was greatly indebted to this patriotic preacher, both for his sentiments and the invincible manner with which he enforced them …

---

17 Slater, *T&L*, 47-49.

Prophecy Concerning Washington

"On the 10th of July, 1755, General Braddock sustained his memorable defeat, and the remnant of his army was saved by the courage and skill of Colonel Washington, then but twenty-three years old. On the 20th of the same month, our moral hero preached a sermon, 'On the defeat of General Braddock, going to Fort DuQuesne.' In this sermon, he calls on all his hearers, in the most impassioned and patriotic term, to show themselves men, Britons, Christians, and to make a noble stand for the blessings they enjoyed. In the same year, he delivered a sermon before Captain Overton's company of volunteers, under the title of 'Religion and patriotism, the constituents of a good soldier.' It was in the discussion of this subject that his famous prophecy occurred. Speaking of the encouraging fact, that God had 'diffused some sparks of martial fire through the country,' said he, 'as a remarkable instance of this, I may point out to the public that heroic youth, Colonel Washington, whom **I cannot but hope Providence has hitherto preserved, in so signal a manner, for some important service to his country.'**

"…True eloquence, like true religion is a movement of sensibility as well as an act of reason. If one has 'thoughts that breathe,' you may be sure he will have 'words that burn.' If one is truly a patriot, in the pulpit or out of it, his conduct will comport with his professions, and **his life will be at the service of his country as well as of his God.**"

Complete the T Chart on Rev. Davies' character qualities.

Internal	External

Part V: America; Fullest Expression of a Christian Nation

Rev. John Witherspoon 1722-1794 — New Jersey[18]

"A happy combination of piety and patriotism, constituting the most useful private and public virtue, we have already found in different sections of our common country during the Revolution. We have only to turn to the highest council of our infant nation, the most august assembly of men that ever congregated to declare themselves free, and we shall find another illustrious example in the person of John Witherspoon.

"He was lineally descended from John Knox, the moral hero of Scotland, was born near Edinburgh, 1722, and from the time he adopted America as his country, was as much distinguished as a preacher as a patriot. Dr. Witherspoon was one of the signers of the Declaration of Independence, which he eloquently defended; through a trying period of congressional responsibility he was a very efficient legislator; and for many years performed the duties of a laborious, erudite, and eminently successful president of Princeton College. On taking his seat in Congress, he surprised his associates, as his brother Davies, had surprised the courts of Virginia, with his wonderful knowledge and skill as a civilian. He was associated with Richard Henry Lee and John Adams on several important committees and himself drew many valuable State papers.... As soon as the liberties of the country were won, Dr. Witherspoon gladly resumed his classical pursuits and the work of the ministry …"

Complete the T Chart on Rev. Witherspoon's character qualities.

Internal	External

---

18 Slater, *T&L*, 49-50.

Restoring the "Idea of America:" the Pulpit

Two things are necessary to restoring the original Christian Constitutional Republic: reformation of the pulpit and reformation of education.

Restoration begins in the pulpit:

The pattern set in Colonial America is as relevant to the needed restoration today as it was then. The Founders put in place a structure of government based upon local self-government that works, because it works not from the top down but from the roots upward.

Restoring the "idea of America" necessarily begins now with the church, with pastors stepping up to their calling, whose "life will be at the service of his country as well as his God," who speaks boldly, and who calls forth the best of American Christians.

"When the age needs great men it will find them—heroes not of the timid mimosa kind, who 'fear the dark cloud, and feel the coming sound.' Preachers in Revolutionary times are **eminently practical**; nature supplies them with abundant ammunition, and necessity teaches them expressly to load and fire.

"They are the flying artillery of 'the sacramental host of God's elect.' They are inspired by no fictitious goddess of the Aonian Mount, but by that Eternal Spirit who directed the pen of Moses, the fingers of David, and the tongue of Paul; they drink of no fancied Pierian spring, but at a purer and more exalted source.... The most highly endowed among men are the chosen medium of communications from heaven.

"It is not to be understood, however, that Dr. Witherspoon, or his distinguished co-patriots in the pulpit, were religious or political fanatics. When a clergyman transforms himself into a frenzied partisan, the dupe or champion of a local faction, he renders himself the more odious in contrast with the exalted profession he has disgraced.... What can be more sacrilegious and fatal to human hopes than to place an earthly passion or human interest on the altar by the side of Christ, and sometimes even in Christ's own place?

"But the appropriate functions of a religious teacher do not forbid the duties of a patriot—they imperiously demand them. God designed that the minister of the Gospel should be the man of the people, the confidant of their miseries, the balm of their secret griefs, the depositary of their tears, the interpreter of their necessities, their protector, friend and father, a living providence to all who hunger and thirst, a light to guide the benighted, and a beacon to warn those in danger of destruction.

"Give me such churches and you give me so many fountains of national life for the Republic—fountains which will send crystal tides of purity and vitality through every artery and vein of our national and sectional government to cleanse and sweeten and heal and vitalize our government."[19]

Restoration then in the classroom

The mindless social engineering called American education today, both public and private, is the outcome of what Rev. Samuel Davies called "a timid ... clergy". In a Republic founded upon Christian principles, those principles must courageously and consistently be taught to the individuals in our churches and to the children in our school rooms. The church must take responsibility for educating its children in whole truth, in the principles of Christianity that translate into government, economics, politics, and social issues. The church can no longer expect or trust that secular, socialistic governance is protecting its religious liberty in America; to do so is faithless and amounts to relinquishing the mandate to proclaim the Gospel. American Christians will answer to God for the blessing of self-government of which they bear stewardship.

---

19 David Gregg, *Makers of the American Republic* (1896), 325.

Restoring Christian Character and Self-Government

The classroom is the fountainhead of restoring Christian character and self-government to the nation. "To educate the children of today is to construct the foundation of the nation of tomorrow. Faithless teaching makes for unfaithful citizens. Shall our nation continue in the faith of our Founding Fathers or shall we veer in the direction of secularizing the citizens of tomorrow? This is not merely one of our nation's problems. It is the problem of all problems, for as we educate our youth today so will be our nation tomorrow.

An American Christian Education

"For over one hundred years Americans have not known or learned of America's Christian History. Five generations of Americans have produced a national ignorance concerning the Providential founding of this nation and of God's hand in preserving, defending, and leading the Colonists to victory in 1775–1781—the seven long years of the American Christian Revolution. Today we have no proud heroes—no models of character, or leadership, to inspire our youth. We have no identity for courage, conscience or compassion, to cherish as part of the proud fabric, which a people weaves into its character and tradition. The reason is not that we do not possess such a treasury of greatness and heroism. The reason is that we have allowed our treasury to be robbed and pillaged of its gold—<u>the gold of Christian character</u>. In so doing we have lost our vision of the destiny and purpose of God's America.

"One hundred years ago we took education out of the Christian home where it had raised up men and women who were God-fearing, Christ-honoring, Bible-loving people. People who were willing to count the cost of Christian liberty. Yielding to the arguments of secularism in the 1830's, 40's and 50's, we permitted our churches to relinquish their leadership of Christian education. In making this change into the government sponsored schools, we closed our Bible as the educational and political textbook, and we shifted our level of education from the building of individual Christian character to the building of a group character, conformable to society. As we shifted from a God-centered republic to a man-centered democracy—we began to flounder.

"Today, while the signs of the times seem most disheartening, there is evidence that the overturning, overturning, overturning, is taking place. Our unique heritage and founding has again been brought to light and some Americans are remembering their Christian heritage. Some Christians are again raising the standard of character and conscience of our Pilgrim, Puritan and Patriot heroes and heroines. The conservative revolution of our times is in effect a Christian revolution. It will force us ultimately to awaken from our national apathy. It will inspire us to build up our individual defenses, and so to strengthen our citadel of freedom—which is the mighty fortress of Christianity itself.

"The Christian school—a direct outgrowth of our Bible-based Christian churches—has a most critical role to play in restoring Christian leadership to our nation. The anti-Christian education of the progressive state schools has produced the socialism and the communism of our times. Teachers are most vital to Christian school education— teachers who are models of Christian character and teachers who are alert to the challenge to America's freedom and the nature of that challenge. <u>Christianity alone is the citadel of America's freedom</u>.

"The Founding Fathers of our nation had a clear conception of Christian character and Christian citizenship as part of the inseparable fabric of education. They cherished both these aspects of development as vital

to the maintenance of individual liberty and the freedom of America. Samuel Adams, that devoted and intrepid Christian, known as the "Father of the American Revolution" urges teachers of the young to give careful consideration to the virtues of Christian character and knowledge of Christian self-government in the following passage, found in the opening pages of Christian History of the Constitution of the United States of America:

> *'Let divines and philosophers, statesmen and patriots, unite their endeavors to renovate the age, by impressing the minds of men with the importance of educating their little boys and girls, of inculcating in the minds of youth the fear and love of the Deity and universal philanthropy, and, in subordination to these great principles, the love of their country; of <u>instructing them in the art of self-government</u>, without which they never can act a wise part in the government of societies, great or small; in short of leading them in the study and practice of the exalted virtues of the Christian system …' Christian History, page XIV*

"The record of America as a Christian nation resides in the documented history of her founding. This record has been deliberately obscured in order to deprive the individual of his Christian heritage of individual liberty. The rediscovery of the Christian foundation of our country will restore the Christian leadership of America. This knowledge needs to be part of the background of every individual engaged in the education of American youth.

"As Christian teachers and parents draw upon their own love of Christ and country they will discover many new ways in which to build a living curriculum from the Christian treasury of the founding of our nation. As the student sees his own relationship to Christianity and to America he can be helped to put into practice Christianity's own form of government—Christian self-government. Emma Willard, a Christian educator, whose biography can be found on pages 438 and 439 of Christian History, makes the following statement in her "Abridged History of the United States: or Republic of America," 1843:

> *'There are those, who rashly speak, as if in despair of the fortunes of our republic; because, say they, political virtue has declined. If so, then is there the more need to infuse patriotism into the breasts of the coming generation. And what is so likely to effect this national self-preservation, as to give our children, for their daily reading and study, such a record of the sublime virtues of the worthies of our earliest day,—and of Washington and his compatriots, as shall leave its due impress? And what but the study of their dangers and toils,—their devotion of life and fortune, can make our posterity know, what our country, and our liberties, have cost? And what but the History of our peculiar, complicated fabric of government, by which it may be examined, as piece by piece the structure was built up, can impart such a knowledge of the powers it gives, and the duties it enjoins, as shall enable our future citizens, to become its enlightened and judicious supporters.'*

Restoring the Republic is achievable; sustaining it over changing generations is more challenging. We dare not fail to sustain it.[20]

Words Have Consequences

Most American Christians are not aware of the deconstruction of American English, much less so the implications of "linguistic relativism." A sign of the times is the theft of original and absolute meaning of words and texts, replaced by "cultural creations" and "social constructions." Therefore we hear euphemisms replacing anything considered "harsh" such as "choice" replacing abortion, or "undocumented" replacing illegal aliens. This deconstruction of meaning with terms like "social justice", "gay", "tolerance", reduces the actual meaning of concepts to a less objectionable character that desensitizes people and whitewashes lawlessness.

---

20 Slater, *T&L*, xiii.

The original Webster dictionary published in 1828 has been called "the Rosetta Stone"[21] that enables Americans to enter into a world lost to us. It allows us to restore vocabulary to its original meaning, think clearly, exercise discernment, and walk free of the assault of cultural contrivance that debases language to get power. For instance, the definition of education exemplifies deconstruction of language. The modern definition reduces education to anything anyone wants it to be. Webster's original definition of education is the foundation stone of the Republic.

New Oxford American Dictionary	Original Webster 1828
EDUCATION |ˌejəˈkāSHən|, noun 1. the process of receiving or giving systematic instruction. • the theory and practice of teaching • a body of knowledge acquired while being educated • information about or training in a particular field or subject	EDUCA′TION, *n.* [L. *educatio.*] The bringing up, as of a child; instruction; formation of manners. Education comprehends all that series of instruction and discipline . . . intended to enlighten the understanding, correct the temper, and form the manners and habits of youth, and fit them for usefulness in their future stations. To give children a good *education* in manners, arts and science, is important; to give them a religious *education* is indispensable; and an immense responsibility rests on parents and guardians who neglect these duties.

Comparing and contrasting the modern and original definition of education in America explains much of what is wrong in our classrooms. It also demonstrates the danger in the deconstruction of language. A major effort to redefine our words from the original source that defined true liberty is essential to restoring the Republic.

Final Essay: "Education for the American Republic"

"Education and the American Republic" What is the role of American education in sustaining a self-governing republic? What are the dangers of neglecting education by leaving it to the social engineering systems of today? What can be done to restore the Republic today? What can you do? Imagine that you are presenting this idea to your pastor or your neighbor. How would you document your thoughts to be persuasive?

Include a brief explanation of the themes or concepts that define the "idea of America:"
  • *The character of liberty*
  • *The principle of individuality*
  • *God's Hand in history*
  • *Natural and revealed law*
  • *The impact of Christ on religion, education, and government*
  • *The role of the pastor and the schoolroom in unifying the colonies to form a union*

---

21 Rebecca H. Beach, "*Abstract and Four Articles: Technometrics of PA, Recovering William Ames, Recovering Peter Ramus, Confront the War on Language—Noah Webster's 1828,*" 2014, MS Sacramento.

Howard Pyle

"Throw your heart into a picture and then jump in after it."

These are the words of Howard Pyle which aptly represent the spirit and passion of the artist- illustrator.

Howard Pyle was born on March 5, 1853 in Wilmington, Delaware. He was an American writer and illustrator. On April 12, 1881 Pyle married singer Anne Poole. They had seven children.

Pyle's best-known work is a unique combination of historical accuracy and his own personal vision. He had a vibrant imagination that allowed stories to come alive with authenticity as well as creativity.

In 1903 Pyle painted The Nation Makers, a reproduction of the life at the front of the Battle of the Brandywine, fought in September 1777. This painting captures the "unbearable charge of intensity" as the figures leap forward with vehemence, expressing how America saw itself in the years before the first World War.

Pyle was widely respected during his life and was highly regarded by illustrators and fine artists. Vincent Van Gogh wrote in a letter to his brother Theo that Pyle's work "struck me dumb with admiration." Pyle was the founder of a distinctly American school of illustration, which became known as the Brandywine School, and was considered an innovator of the total-design approach. Howard Pyle died on November 9, 1911 in Florence, Italy.

Bibliography

Adams, George Burton and H. Morse Stephens, Eds. *Select Documents of English Constitutional History*. New York: The MacMillan Co., 1901.

Ames, William. *The Marrow of Theology*. Durham, NC: The Labyrinth Press, 1968.

Beach, Rebecca H. *Abstract and Four Articles: Technometrics of PA, Recovering William Ames, Recovering Peter Ramus, Confront the War on Language — Noah Webster's 1828*. 2014. MS, Sacramento.

Beach, Rebecca H., and Carole G. Adams. *Finding the Real Common Core of American Christian Education: The Theology of American Liberty*. Speech, Reason for Hope, Virginia, Virginia Beach, February 11, 2015.

Beach, Rebecca H. *The Goodness and the Liberty of the Two and the Ten*. 2016. MS, Sacramento.

Foxe, John. *Foxe's Book of Martyrs*. Grand Rapids, MI: Fleming H. Revell, 1998.

Graves, Frank Pierrepont Graves. *Peter Ramus and the Educational Reformation of the Sixteenth Century*. New York: The MacMillan Co., 1912

Gregg, David. *Makers of the American Republic*. New York: E.B. Treat, 1896.

Hall, Edwin. *The Puritans and their Principles*. New York: Baker & Scribner, 1846.

Hall, Verna M. *The Christian History of the Constitution of the United States of America: Christian Self-Government*. Chesapeake, VA: Foundation for American Christian Education, 2014.

Hall, Verna M. *The Christian History of the American Revolution: Consider and Ponder*. San Francisco: Foundation for American Christian Education, 1976.

Lord, John. *Beacon Lights of History, Vol. II*. New York: Fords, Howard, and Hulbert, 1884.

Malone, Dumas and William H. B. Thomas. *A Miracle of Virginia: The School for Statesmen*. Charlottesville, VA: Ben Franklin Publishing, 1984.

Ong, Walter J. *"Homiletic," Journal of the History of Ideas*, 14, (1953) 235-248.

Rose, James B. "Peter Ramus and William Ames: French and English Precursors to the Principle Approach." The Journal of the Foundation for American Christian Education VI (1994-1995): 13-21.

Slater, Rosalie J. *Teaching and Learning America's Christian History: The Principle Approach*. Chesapeake, VA: Foundation for American Christian Education, 2017.

Sprunger, Keith L. *The Learned Doctor William Ames: Dutch Backgrounds of English and American Puritanism*. Chicago: University of Illinois Press, 1972.

Webster, Noah. *The American Dictionary of the English Language*. Facsimile of the original 1828 publication. Chesapeake, VA: Foundation for American Christian Education, 2016.

Willard, Emma. *Universal History in Perspective: Divided into Three Parts, Ancient, Middle, and Modern*. New York: A.S. Barnes & Co., 1855.

Index of Images

Page 13 Noah Webster Painted by Edwin B. Childs 1933 Merriam-Webster, Inc.

Page 14 A View of the Buildings of Yale College at New Haven By Amos Doolittle

Page 14 Mount Vernon, home of George Washington

Page 22 Washington Refusing a Dictatorship By Howard Pyle, Father of American Illustration, From Harper's Magazine, October, 1883

Page 29 A Lonely Duel in the Middle of a Great Sunny Field By Howard Pyle Father of American Illustration

Page 33 John Quincy Adams By John Singleton Copley, Museum of Fine Arts, Boston

Page 38 Committee of Franklin, Jefferson, Adams, Livingston, and Sherman Consulting on the Declaration of Independence. Virginia Historical Society

Page 40 Nation Makers By Howard Pyle, Brandywine Museum, Pennsylvania.

Page 43 The Baptism of Pocahontas by John G. Chapman (1842) Mural in the Capitol Rotunda, Washington, D.C.

Page 54 The Dove Sent Forth From the Ark, by Gustave Dore'

Page 65 The Ten Commandments

Page 66 The Holy Experiment: Our Heritage from William Penn, by Violet Oakley (student of Howard Pyle) Limited edition book of her line drawings, Cogslea Studio Publications (1950), From her mural paintings in the State Capitol, Harrisburg, Pennsylvania

Page 68 The Child Moses on the Nile, by Gustave Dore'

Page 75 Murder of Cicero

Page 78 Homer Reciting the Iliad

Page 80 Arch of Constantine

Page 86 Writing the Declaration of Independence, 1776 By Jean Leon Gerome Ferris, Virginia Historical Society

Page 89 Wiclif Writing, Harper's Magazine, Jan. 1885, Vol. LXX, No. CCCCXVI

Page 92 Dawn: Luther at Erfurt By Joseph Noel Patton National Galleries of Scotland, Edinburgh, United Kingdom (1861)

Page 93 Luther Bible

Page 94 Luther Songbook, Lutherhaus Museum, Wittenberg, Germany Photographed by Paul T. McCain

Page 95 Portrait of a Man

Page 97 The Holy Experiment: Our Heritage from William Penn, by Violet Oakley (student of Howard Pyle) Limited edition book of her line drawings, Cogslea Studio Publications (1950), From her mural paintings in the State Capitol, Harrisburg, Pennsylvania

Page 100 William Tyndale Imprisoned

Page 101 William Tyndale Strangled and Burned

Page 102 Peter Ramus

Page 104 King John from De Rege Johanne

Page 105 Magna Charta signed by King John at Runneymeade 1215 . Photo by Jon Chase/Harvard University

Page 115 John Locke By Godfrey Kneller

Page 117 Portrait of Montesquieu Palace of Versailles (1728)

Page 119 Sir William Blackstone National Portrait Gallery

Page 126 The Burning of James Towne By Howard Pyle

Page 127 John Smith's Map of Virginia

Page 129 The state's motto "Sic Semper Tyrannis" means "Thus Always to Tyrants." The seal was approved at Virginia's 1776 Constitutional Convention, and the principal designer is said to have been George Wythe.

Page 131 John Robinson sending the Pilgrims to America

Page 132 John Elliot, The First Missionary among the Indians Painted by J.A. Oertel, History of the United States by J.A. Spencer, Johnson, Fry and Company, New York (1866)

Page 133 William Ames By Gustavus Ellinthorpe Sintzenich

Page 135 Rev Samuel Davies

Page 137 John Witherspoon Princeton University Art Museum

Page 142 Howard Pyle in his art studio

Part V: America; Fullest Expression of a Christian Nation